"PEACE, LAND, BREAD!"

WORLD HISTORY LIBRARY

"PEACE, LAND, BREAD!"
A HISTORY OF
THE RUSSIAN
REVOLUTION

JOHN J. VAIL

Facts On File, Inc.
AN INFOBASE HOLDINGS COMPANY

On the Cover: March 8—Women's Emancipation Days. Poster, 1920, by Adolf Strakhov

"Peace, Land, Bread!" A History of the Russian Revolution

Facts On File, Inc
11 Penn Plaza
New York NY 10001

Library of Congress Cataloging-in-Publication Data

Vail, John J.
　"Peace, land, bread!" : a history of the Russian Revolution / John
J. Vail.
　　　p.　cm. — (World history library)
　　Includes bibliographical references and index.
　　ISBN 0-8160-2818-4 (alk. paper)
　　1. Soviet Union—History—Revolution, 1917–1921—Juvenile
literature.　2. Russia—History—Nicholas II, 1894–1917—Juvenile
literature.　[1. Soviet Union—History—Revolution, 1917–1921.
2. Russia—History—Nicholas II, 1894–1917.]　I. Title.
II. Series.
　　DK265.V167　1995
　　947.084'1—dc20　　　　　　　　　　　94-26634

Facts On File books are available at special discounts when purchased in bulk quantities for businesses, associations, institutions or sales promotions. Please call our Special Sales Department in New York at 212/967-8800 or 800/322-8755.

Text design by Donna Sinisgalli
Cover design by Amy Beth Gonzalez
Maps by Dale Williams

Printed in the United States of America

MP FOF 10 9 8 7 6 5 4 3 2 1

This book is printed on acid-free paper.

To Luke, Martin, and Will
May their generation see
their dreams realized

CONTENTS

PREFACE

Revolutions are exceptional moments in human history, when ordinary citizens suddenly leap onto the historical stage and become transformed from passive subjects into historical actors. Within a matter of days, a revolution can overturn hundreds of years of history and pave the way for change of lasting world importance. The Russian Revolution of 1917 was the most momentous social and political upheaval since the American and French Revolutions of the late 18th century. It unleashed a seismic upheaval that dramatically reshaped the fate of Russia and the world of the 20th century.

The Russian Revolution was actually a series of successive upheavals, each building upon and transforming those that preceded it. In February 1917, five days of protests by the workers and soldiers of Petrograd overturned the 300-year-old Romanov dynasty and began the creation of a constitutional order. A provisional government attempted to govern the country and guide the Revolution along a moderate track. A crippling economic crisis, discontent with a bankrupt policy that committed Russia to a disastrous war, and deepening social polarization led to a growing radicalization of the Russian masses. They turned to the Bolshevik party, whose program of "Peace, Bread, and Land" attracted enormous support from Russia's workers, soldiers, and peasants. The Bolsheviks organized the October 1917 Revolution, which overthrew the Provisional Government and established a Soviet government. The Soviet regime would in turn be engulfed in a horrifying civil war that devastated Russia and irrevocably altered the course of the Revolution.

"Peace, Land and Bread!": A History of the Russian Revolution will explore the dramatic events of this heady passage from the February Revolution to Red October to civil war: the rise and fall of the fortunes of political figures and parties, the downfall of the Provisional Government and the triumph of the Bolsheviks, the aspirations of the Russian masses who propelled the Revolution forward, and the betrayal of the dreams of 1917 in the wake of the cataclysm of civil war.

It is indeed the Russian masses who will be at the forefront of the story. The Russian Revolution was first and foremost a profound struggle and deep yearning on the part of the Russian people for freedom and democracy in their daily lives. They were convinced that the best way to regain control over their lives was to overthrow everything that oppressed, degraded, and humiliated them and to expand democratic decision-making over every aspect of their lives. The Revolution was a remarkable testament to a vision of the world that insisted that every individual was capable of, and could aspire to, a life of purpose and creativity. It became a beacon of hope for the downtrodden and exploited in Russia and for people throughout the world who also dreamed of transforming their lives. It is in this sense that the main drama of the Russian Revolution was not the actions of the "great men of history," but rather those of ordinary men and women, the anonymous workers, soldiers, sailors, and peasants of Russia who seized center stage of history.

The issue of historical alternatives will also play an important role in the story of the Revolution. Many historians have maintained that there was a fundamental continuity, if not an inevitable link, between the Bolshevik seizure of power in October 1917 and the subsequent development of a totalitarian dictatorship in Russia. However, there are always historical alternatives: without an investigation of what might have been possible in history, an honest appraisal of the past is impossible. The evolution of the Russian Revolution was not the outcome of some conspiratorial plan or the inescapable fate of an original sin as portrayed in Shakespearean tragedy. It was the complex product of great social upheavals, economic catastrophes, and political miscalculations that had profound, if unforeseen, consequences. There are always critical turning points in history, periods where a promising future can be swept away in favor of horrible alternatives, and the Russian Civil War was such a moment in the history of the Russian Revolution. It was to exert an inordinate influence on the course of the Revolution, dooming the hopes for a new world based on justice, democracy, and freedom that had so fired the imagination of 1917.

With the recent demise of Communist governments in Russia and Eastern Europe, many observers have been tempted to argue that we have reached an "end of history." They believe that the problems and concerns that animated the Russian revolutionaries have been resolved once and for all by the triumph of liberal democracy and capitalism throughout the world. It is said that the Russian Revolution, now seemingly relegated to a mere footnote in history, no longer has historical significance or contemporary relevance. Yet, a critical appreciation of the world today reveals the inescapable conclusion that poverty, inequality, exploitation, environmental degradation, and racial and gender oppression continue to flourish. The fundamental challenge that the Russian revolutionaries posed back in 1917, of creating conditions that enable ordinary people to live lives of decency and dignity, remains unrealized at the end of the 20th century, and it is for this reason that the Revolutionary spirit of 1917 will continue to inspire and empower future generations of the 21st century.

CHAPTER 1

RUSSIA UNDER THE TSARS

Even when considered against the backdrop of Russia's tumultuous history of the late 19th and early 20th centuries, the events of 1894 would prove to be memorable. The city of Moscow had been in a state of feverish preparations for months in anticipation of the coronation of Nicholas II as the tsar (supreme ruler) of all Russia in May. Buildings had been scrubbed and repainted, new trees had been planted along all the major boulevards, and colorful bunting and banners decorated every window. The most exclusive private clubs and restaurants hosted sumptuous dinner parties and lavish balls for the country's nobles and elites. Special performances of the Bolshoi Ballet and the Imperial Theater were mounted in celebration of the monarchy, with tickets fetching prices above what an average Muscovite earned in an entire year.

The official ceremonies began on May 9 with the traditional entrance of the monarch into the ancient capital. The 28-year-old Nicholas rode along the imperial route atop a magnificent white stallion. Behind him in a long procession rode the princes and counts of the imperial family, flanked by majestically decorated honor guards. An ornate gold carriage, drawn by a team of eight white horses, carried the Tsarina Alexandra, Nicholas's young bride. Five days after this triumphal entrance, Nicholas became the eighteenth member of the Romanov dynasty to be crowned tsar of Russia.

That same evening, 7,000 guests were treated to an extraordinary banquet and gala dance in Nicholas and Alexandra's honor. Tables overflowed with expensive wine, champagne, caviar, and other Russian delicacies. The tsar, however, was concerned that every one of his subjects should enjoy his coronation, so a gigantic outdoor festival was also planned for the Russian people at the vast Khodynka Field, where the Russian army practiced its maneuvers and entrenchments. Great mounds of food were to be laid out alongside stands that would serve bountiful quantities of beer and wine. In the days leading up to the celebration, huge crowds of peasants and workers from all over the country poured into Moscow. For people whose daily fare typically consisted of cabbage soup and bread crusts, such a feast could hardly be imagined.

By the morning of the festival, nearly half a million people were gathered near the fairgrounds. Only a handful of police had been assigned to crowd control, and they struggled to keep some semblance of order. Every person was eager to be among the first to sample the tsar's generosity, and they pressed forward with an irresistible momentum. Suddenly, the massive crowd broke through the makeshift barriers and surged onto the field. Within minutes the scene was transformed into a nightmarish stampede. Wave after wave was propelled into the ditches and trenches left behind by the military. Scores of people were trampled to death in the mad rush or were crushed under the tremendous weight of bodies. By early afternoon, the grounds were nearly empty, the food and drink lay untouched, and thousands of broken, battered bodies littered the landscape. Five thousand people were killed and an equal number wounded in the disaster.

Throughout the morning's events, at the other end of Khodynka Field, a stand containing the royal family, nobles, army officers, and foreign guests were serenaded by a children's choir and were warmly greeted by the tsar and tsarina, both of whom were blissfully unaware of the horrors that had engulfed people just a short distance away. As a result of the tragedy, the tsar's confidants urged him to cancel the remaining coronation events, yet Nicholas decided to carry on as if sanctioned. Every tsar or tsarina believed with absolute certainty that he or she had been chosen by the hand of God to lead the nation. Russia's autocrats exercised total control over the country's fortunes: they appointed all ministers, approved all decisions, dominated all policy-making. Until 1905, there were no elections, no political parties to contest their rule, no legislature to overturn their decrees. The press was strictly censored and civil liberties were nonexistent. The tsar's word was law, and he expected the total submission of his subjects.

The tsar's authority rested on three major pillars: the bureaucracy, the Orthodox church, and the police and army. Together they helped ensure the legitimacy and stability of the regime. The first of these, the bureaucracy, was a pervasive feature of Russian society. From the moment the empire was formed, the administration of the vast territory was entrusted to a "civilian priesthood," organized in a massive, hierarchical organization, consisting of 14 ranks (or ladders). At the top of the pyramid were the nobility, the largest landowners in the country, who were obliged to provide permanent service to the tsar. They served primarily as cabinet ministers, running various governmental departments and serving as the personal staff of the monarch. They served at the tsar's pleasure and could be dismissed at his whim. The lower ranks of the bureaucracy were composed of poorly paid civil servants who also pledged an oath of blind obedience to the tsar, as well as unquestioning acceptance of the orders of their superiors.

The Orthodox church was the second underpinning of the tsarist edifice. Descended from the Greek Orthodox branch of Christianity, its primary function was to legitimate the tsar's reign and lend credence to the status quo. Church officials claimed that the tsar was the vicar of Christ on earth and that disobedience of his commands was a sin. In the church's primary schools and pulpits, priests taught that tsarism was permanent, unchanging, and unchangeable.

The third pillar of the tsarist system was the brute force and terror of the police and army. The very notion of freedom was incompatible with tsarism: political meetings were broken up, dissidents were subject to arbitrary harassment and imprisonment, opponents were hounded into exile. The Okhrana (tsarist secret police) operated a vast nothing had occurred. He and Alexandra attended several balls during the week, and eight days later, Nicholas presided over a grand finale on the very grounds that had witnessed the shedding of so much innocent blood.

It was an inauspicious beginning to Nicholas's regime yet altogether fitting in its symbolism. Nicholas's government bore ultimate responsibility for the tragedy: for failing to provide an adequate number of police, for leaving the trenches unfilled, for denying the very importance of the events in the hearts and minds of Russians. It was Nicholas's government that would lead his ill-prepared nation into a bloody and disastrous world war. It was Nicholas's government that would lie broken and battered less than a quarter of a century later, torn apart by war and revolution. The tsar's personal tragedy was that he would greet his last moments in power with the same telling indifference that marked his first.

THE TSARIST SYSTEM

By the end of the 19th century, the Romanovs had been the supreme rulers of Russia for an unbroken stretch dating back to the 1600s. They commanded a vast empire reaching from Poland in the west to the Pacific Ocean in the east, from the Arctic Ocean in the north to the Black Sea in the south. Yet when measured against the development of other countries in Europe, Russia was in every respect a backward nation. While the spirit of liberal democracy had begun to spread its message across the face of Europe, Russia remained under the control of a single monarch unchecked by anyone. While other European countries had made breathtaking leaps in living standards and public education, the bulk of Russia's populace was still trapped in poverty and ignorance. While traditions in the rest of Europe were crumbling rapidly under the pressure of progress, Russia seemed as entrenched in its old ways as ever before. Indeed, tsarism appeared totally resistant to change, and few would have guessed that its demise was just a short time away.

The centerpiece of the Russian autocracy (monarchy) was the tsar himself. From the reign of Peter the Great (1689–1725) through Catherine the Great (1762–1796) and Alexander I (1801–1825), Russia's rulers were considered all powerful, unchallengeable and divinely masters and tax collectors. Peasant revolts against this oppression were commonplace but were routinely crushed by tsarist troops.

Traditional farming practices in Russia under serfdom were economically unproductive as well. The peasant commune (*mir*), or village assembly, decided patterns of cultivation and allocations of land for all members of the village. It divided various qualities among all the households in the village, ensuring that every household had plots of equal quality and a share that corresponded to the size of their family. However, these plots might be so scattered across the countryside that it would take peasants an hour to walk from their home to their land. Their property was often so narrow that there was hardly enough room to turn a plow. Almost all of the work on the farm was done by hand. Peasants used wooden plows to till the land and hand sickles to cut their crops. They lacked sophisticated irrigation systems or agricultural machinery. Because the peasants did not own their own land, there was no reason for them to improve productivity, especially when the resulting profits would accrue to the landlords and not the peasants themselves.

As part of a wider program of political and social reforms, Alexander II issued the Emancipation Acts in 1860 that freed the serfs. Peasants were now at liberty to marry as they pleased, move wherever they wanted, and buy and sell property. The reforms were expected to act as an incentive for greater productivity and to decrease dissent among the peasantry, but they proved a mixed blessing. Every peasant was burdened by stiff redemption payments to the government, which were used to compensate the peasant's former owners. Few peasants had the money to purchase enough land on which to make a comfortable living. The vast majority received little or no property at all as a result of their new freedom. Nor did productivity improve dramatically: the dominance of the mir went unchallenged and would-be enterprising peasants were still unable to either consolidate or expand their holdings. The techniques and tools of farming remained backward and virtually nothing was done to instruct peasants in new agricultural techniques. The failure to either alleviate the roots of peasant discontent or to provide a firm foundation for greater economic growth would have severe repercussions for the tsarist regime.

THE GOLDEN AGE OF RUSSIAN LITERATURE

The 19th century was the golden age of Russian literature. Writers such as Ivan Turgenev, Fyodor Dostoevsky, Leo Tolstoy, and Anton Chekhov produced an extraordinary outpouring of novels, poems, short stories, and plays that offered a vivid portrait and critique of the very fabric of tsarist society.

In 1852, the same year that Harriet Beecher Stowe published *Uncle Tom's Cabin*, an impassioned indictment of slavery in the United States, Turgenev published *Notes of a Huntsman*, a poignant description of the lives of the Russian serfs, which sparked a similar abolitionist fervor in Russia. His moving sketches illustrated that the peasantry were not the undistinguished mass so often depicted in Russian literature, but rather lived an existence filled with sorrow, suffering, happiness, and dignity, equal in drama and significance to that of any aristocratic family. Turgenev also wrote sympathetically of the new generation of Russian youth who were offering a radical challenge to tsarism. Evgeny Bazarov, the central character of his brilliant novel *Fathers and Sons*, was described as a nihilist, a person who "does not bow before any authority and who accepts nothing on faith." Barazov accepted as a matter of principle the radical belief that there was not "a single convention in our present day family or civic life that does not demand complete and merciless rejection." The revolutionaries of *Fathers and Sons*, coming of age after Russia's devastating defeat in the Crimean War, believed the key to Russia's future lay in the relentless advancement of science and technology, which alone could transform backward Russia.

Dostoevsky experienced firsthand the cost of a commitment to radical politics. At the age of 28, he was sentenced to death for his role in a revolutionary conspiracy; he was taken before a firing squad and blindfolded, and the orders to prepare for firing were given—then, at the very last second, a reprieve was granted. Dostoevsky never quite recovered from the ordeal: he endured four arduous years at prison labor in Siberia, and upon his release, his hatred of revolutionary politics was matched only by his espousal of Christian love and devotion as the answer to Russia's predicament. The central theme of his great novels *Crime and Punishment*, *The Devils*, and *The Brothers Karamazov* explored the difficulties individuals faced in achieving a life of salvation and indeed what salvation actually meant in the context of 19th-century Russia.

The central figure of *Crime and Punishment*, Raskolnikov, is a poor student who considers himself to be an elite by virtue of his superior intellect and vision and who believes he is outside society and the laws that bind ordinary humans. To prove himself worthy to be one of these supermen, Raskolnikov brutally murders an old woman pawnbroker but discovers that his heinous act leads not to personal transcendence but rather to desperation and tragedy. The revolutionaries depicted in *The Devils* all reach a similar dead end: the most intelligent and capable of them, Stavrogin, is unable to find any sense of worth or hope of redemption through his activities and ends up hanging himself. The three brothers in his greatest work, *The Brothers Karamazov*, take different paths to enlightenment—Ivan looks to European ideas, Dimitri to personal wealth, and Alyosha to the self-sacrifice of Christianity—yet none succeed or provide any hope for other Russians. The depth of Dostoevsky's pessimistic vision is demonstrated in the chapter in which the Grand Inquisitor confronts Christ, who has returned to earth. The Inquisitor informs him that the modern Church has retreated from his preaching about love and goodness in order to better account for the debased roots of human nature: "We have corrected your work and based it upon miracle, mystery and authority," a new trinity that corresponded to the dead weight of autocracy and orthodoxy in Russian society.

In *The Cherry Orchard*, Chekhov, Russia's foremost playwright, explored the confrontation between the old order and the new modern Russia that emerged after 1860. He compared the dying aristocracy, exemplified by the aristocratic widow, Madame Rarevskaya, with the dynamic new wealth and energy of the bourgeoisie and industrialists. Madame Rarevskaya faces ultimate ruin because of her wasteful lifestyle and her inability to adjust to the changing world. Lapakhin, a former servant who has made his fortune in the new market climate, offers her a way of saving her home but at a steep price: he proposes to cut down the estates' vast cherry orchard in order to subdivide the land into smaller parcels to sell as summer cottages for the urban bourgeoisie. The widow rejects the idea as "hopelessly vulgar" and does nothing, leaving the way clear for Lapakhin to buy up the estate and implement the destruction of the orchard. The play is a marvelously evocative account of the indecisiveness and complacency that ultimately doom the aristocracy.

Tolstoy, often considered to be Russia's greatest novelist, was an impassioned foe of the Romanov regime for the last three decades of his life. His epic novels *War and Peace* and *Anna Karenina* brilliantly portray the life and culture of the Russian elite, and his later short stories and novels, such as *Resurrection*, are unsparing in their criticism of tsarist institutions. In 1892, convinced that the autocracy had refused to recognize the depths of discontent within the nation, he wrote a famous open letter to the tsar in which he urged Nicholas "to give the masses the opportunity to express their desires and demands." The autocracy no longer answers to the needs of the Russian people, concluded the novelist.

MODERNIZATION AND THE WORKERS

In the early 1880s, Russia launched a crash program in industrialization to ensure its status as a world power. With the aid of massive government financing and foreign investment, entire new industries in iron and steel, chemicals, petroleum, and engineering were created almost overnight. Within three decades, Russia became the fifth largest industrial power in the world. This rapid industrial takeoff had profound social consequences. A small class of business elites (also known as the bourgeoisie) emerged to manage and control these new industrial enterprises. Although still a tiny percentage of the nation's population,

Russia's working class also grew in leaps and bounds, reaching 3.4 million workers nationwide in 1914. In the industrial heartland of St. Petersburg, the total jumped from 73,000 in 1890 to 245,000 in 1917.

Workers lived in squalid districts typically located on the outskirts of a city. Sanitary conditions were appalling: nearly two thirds of all homes lacked sewerage facilities or their own water supply. Open cesspools were everywhere and garbage piled up uncollected in the streets. Roads were unpaved and turned into muddy quagmires in the winter. Workers were crammed into incredibly overcrowded surroundings, with two or three families forced to live together in a single apartment. Indeed overcrowding was so bad that residents of the Vyborg District in the capital joked that they had even less space than those buried in the nearby cemetery.

Wages were so low that most workers could barely afford the bare necessities of life. Women workers were doubly disadvantaged, having to face the toil of work at both the factory floor and at home. One female textile worker complained:

> Having finished work at the factory, the woman worker is still not free. While the male worker goes off to a meeting or just takes a walk or plays billiards with his friends, she has to cope with the housework—to cook, to wash and so on . . . she is seldom helped by her husband. Unfortunately, one has to admit that male workers are still very prejudiced. They think it is humiliating for a man to do "women's work." They would sooner their sick, worn out wife did the household chores by herself.

Life inside Russia's factories was extremely harsh. Adult workers rarely worked less than 11 hours a day (children worked 9 hours), with only Sundays off. They faced horrible conditions on the shop floor: workers were exposed to all sorts of harmful chemicals and had to work without masks or ventilation. "In the plant where they do the washing and spraying," one woman at a metal working plant said, "the air is so suffocating and poisonous that someone unused to it could not stand it for more than 10–15 minutes. Your whole body becomes poisoned by it." Disease, poverty, and sickness took a fearful toll. Russian workers literally worked themselves to death. The annual mortality rate in working-class neighborhoods was 24.8 per 1,000 people, compared with 8.7 in upper class residential districts.

Employers ruled their factories as the tsar ruled the country—through absolute fear. Workers were answerable to the petty injustices of foremen who exercised power in an arbitrary fashion. They hired and fired at whim, prevented workers from reading newspapers or political pamphlets, and punished anyone who showed the slightest disobedience. Workers were treated like slaves and faced constant humiliation and mistreatment. Workers had no legal recourse or protection against their employers; they were prevented from joining unions until 1905; and strikes to win better wages or working conditions were severely repressed. Nevertheless, Russian workers were exceptionally militant and highly politically conscious. The historical importance of Russian workers, who represented only a small proportion of the population, was quite disproportionate to their numerical strength. They were destined to play the leading role in the coming revolution.

MODERNIZATION AND POLITICAL REFORM

The broad program of social and economic modernization necessitated political changes as well, though these would have only a limited impact on the fundamental nature of the autocracy. The great reformer Alexander II provided for the reorganization of the judiciary, the introduction of universal military service, and the establishment of a modern military. The state administration was likewise modernized. New institutions of local government, known as *zemstvos*, were enacted across Russia's villages. They were conceived as a means of making the tsarist bureaucracy more efficient and were given responsibility for local services such as public health, education or relief for the poor. Zemstvo officials were recruited from among the local populace and earned a certain degree of autonomy from tsarist control.

Although the zemstvo movement helped plant the seed of political change, the spread of liberal democracy was to remain fatally weak in Russia. This was in part a result of the different social composition of Russian life. Russia's business elites were a relatively small group numerically; unlike their British or French counterparts, who had both material and ideological reasons for opposing their monarchies, they owed their very status and privileges to the tsarist government's initiatives. As a result, they were not politically active and with rare exceptions, fervently embraced the principle of the monarchy. Calls for greater liberal reform were largely the result of pressure by the intelligentsia, a small group drawn from liberal sections of the nobility, writers, political journalists, and the professionals in law, teaching, and medicine. Although the intelligentsia was united in their opposition to the autocracy, they were fatally divided over tactics and goals. Liberal opposition never moved beyond individual protest and discontent into a mass movement; indeed, the Russian liberal party, the Constitutional Democrats (Kadets), did not form until 1905.

The fervent opposition of the autocracy to liberalism also played an important role. Tsarism was structurally and ideologically unable to cooperate with or even accommodate reform. Nicholas contemptuously dismissed all talk of liberal reform as "senseless dreamings." "Let it be known," the tsar warned, "that I will maintain the principle of the autocracy as strongly and firmly as my late memorable Father." Those Russians who were committed to political change seemingly had no choice but to be drawn into the ranks of Russia's revolutionary movements.

CHAPTER ONE NOTES

p. 6   "Be more autocratic . . ." Tsarina Alexandra, quoted in Marcel Liebman. *The Russian Revolution* (New York: Vintage, 1970), p. 22.

p. 11   "Having finished work at the factory . . ." Quoted in S. A. Smith. *Red Petrograd: Revolution in the Factories 1917–1918* (Cambridge: Cambridge University Press, 1983), p. 26.

p. 11   "In the plant where they . . . " Quoted in Smith, p. 41.

RUSSIA OF THE REVOLUTIONARIES

Every unjust and exploitative political system in history, including tsarist Russia, has inevitably engendered a significant resistance to its reign. Indeed, the stubborn determination of the tsars to preserve their illegitimate power was rivaled only by the equally unflinching will of Russian revolutionaries to bring about a just society. The last 50 years of tsarism can be aptly characterized as an ongoing confrontation between the repressive authorities and the thousands of activists who dedicated their lives to defeating the system.

POPULISM

One of the first major streams of the revolutionary movement was populism, which dominated Russian radicalism from the 1860s to the 1880s. The Populists consisted primarily of educated elites and the disillusioned sons and daughters of government bureaucrats. They rejected the aspirations of modern, westernized Russia, which they saw as a wasteland of alienation, hopelessness, and degradation. Instead of looking to the West for visions of a better life, they insisted that social change had to be based on Russia's traditional institutions. The Populists romanticized the primitive peasant commune as the embodiment of all the virtues of an ideal social order. This innocent life was now seriously endangered by the spread of capitalist progress in Russia:

peasants were being uprooted from their land, forced to live in hovels and trapped in a vicious cycle of poverty.

The Populists were convinced that, with sufficient education and propaganda, the people (*narod*) would realize that their situation was intolerable and would have an incentive to cast off the chains of their oppression. They hoped to harness this energy to build a movement among the peasants that could overthrow tsarism. This belief in the people would prove to be the Populists' greatest strength and their greatest weakness. The very people they placed their revolutionary hopes in refused to behave in the way that the revolutionaries predicted or expected.

The Populists first national campaign, the "to the people" movement, was launched in the summer of 1873. Thousands of students and members of the intelligentsia, who felt their place was among the oppressed, left the comfort of their urban existence to "go to the people." They flocked to peasant villages to serve as teachers, agricultural experts, nurses, and doctors. Some hoped to acquire the simple wisdom of the peasants, others to build a revolutionary organization among the masses. All knew they risked arrest, prison, and exile, but they accepted these risks anyway.

The campaign proved to be a complete disaster. Participants were scattered throughout Russia with little coordination and there was no clearly defined political goal or central ideological message. What made matters worse was the Populists' naiveté, their innocent confidence that the peasants would welcome them with open arms. Not surprisingly, the peasants distrusted the intellectuals and misunderstood their motives. They saw the activists as troublemakers who might jeopardize their fragile relationship with the landlords and authorities and as privileged dreamers who knew nothing about the harsh realities of their lives. Revolutionary pamphlets were torn up and used for making homemade cigarettes, and peasants routinely handed over their unwanted guests to the police. The government rounded up most of the movement's participants within a few months and banished all of them to long prison sentences.

The utter failure of their campaign was a devastating blow to the Populists and forced them to reevaluate their strategy. Many were convinced that the only way forward was to embrace the use of political terror as a program. They concluded that the peasants were far too trusting in the tsar's goodwill, too brainwashed in their acceptance of the permanence of the autocratic system, to ever choose rebellion spontaneously. Only with the assassination of the autocracy's leaders would the masses be persuaded that the state could be overthrown.

A wave of terrorism, led by the People's Will, the name of this new terror organization, swept over Russia from 1879–81. The terrorists assassinated police officers, regional governors, and local government officials. Eight assassination attempts were mounted against Alexander II, each involving elaborate and careful plans and preparations and each featuring narrow misses. Finally, on March 1, 1881, while the tsar was traveling to the Winter Palace, a bomb was thrown at his sleigh. He was miraculously unhurt and went to talk to the injured bystanders, whereupon he was mortally wounded by another bomb.

The assassination went horribly wrong: the terrorist leaders expected that the deed would spark a ferocious upheaval, but Russia's masses maintained a stony silence. The terrible irony was that the terrorists believed they were acting in the name of the masses, that they represented the people's will, yet they sought to kill the very symbol to which the masses clung with ever increasing faith. The autocracy was not fatally damaged by the death of its leader. Alexander III proved to be even more reactionary and uncompromising than his predecessor, and he clamped down furiously on all forms of dissent and political activity. Tsarist Russia moved closer to becoming a total police state than ever before. The leaders of the conspiracy were arrested and went to their deaths on the gallows.

The last gasp of the Populists' legacy came in 1887. A plot to assassinate Alexander III was discovered and the culprits were quickly apprehended. One of those arrested was a 19-year-old revolutionary who told his jailers: "There is no better way of dying than to lay down one's life for one's country. Such a death does not fill honest and sincere men with any fear. I have had but one aim: to serve the unfortunate Russian people." The young man, whose name was Alexander Ulyanov, was hanged three days later. His younger brother Vladimir, whom he had won over to revolutionary politics, became known in history as the leader of the Russian Revolution under his pseudonym, Lenin.

VLADIMIR LENIN

Vladimir Lenin, whose real name was Vladimir Ulyanov, was the leader of the Bolshevik party and the first head of the Soviet government formed after the October Revolution of 1917. He was born in Simbirsk in 1870, the son of a respected civil servant. The young Ulyanov grew up in comfortable surroundings: his family spent summers at a cousin's country estate, where the young boy played games and swam with his siblings. It was his older brother Alexander, executed for his role in the assassination plot against Tsar Alexander III, who inspired Lenin to a life of politics. After graduating at the top of his high school class, Lenin entered the University of Kazan and was immediately embroiled in the wave of student protests that ignited Russian campuses in the 1880s. Upon being arrested at one such demonstration, one of the arresting officers asked the young Lenin why he was rebelling. "After all, there is a wall in front of you," said the policeman. "That wall is tottering, you only have to push it for it to fall over," said Lenin. He was expelled from the university for his political activities but eventually received an honors degree in law from St. Petersburg University in 1891.

Lenin's political career began in 1893, when he helped form an organization known as the Union of Struggle to help embolden workers in their struggles against their employers. He was arrested two years later and, like most Russian revolutionaries, was exiled for three years to Siberia. Lenin's sojourn was nowhere near as harsh as that of many of his contemporaries: surrounded by books, journals, and even foreign newspapers, he immersed himself in study and writing. Lenin smuggled out an endless stream of articles and pamphlets and wrote a number of important works, including *The Development of Capitalism in Russia*. It was in exile that he met his longtime companion Nadezhda Krupskaya.

RUSSIAN SOCIAL DEMOCRACY

In the aftermath of the Populist fiascos, Marxism emerged as an influential trend within the revolutionary intelligentsia in the 1880s.

Except for a brief period spent in Russia during the Revolution of 1905, Lenin lived abroad for all the years leading up to the 1917 Revolution. The primary organizer and inspiration of the Bolshevik party, Lenin was also an accomplished and prolific writer, publishing numerous scholarly texts in economic history, philosophy, and politics. One of his first political pamphlets, *What Is to Be Done* (1902), was an attempt to adopt Marxism to the specific historical circumstances of Russia in the early 20th century. Lenin maintained that the workers movement required a highly organized, tightly disciplined political party in order to achieve a revolution in the harsh, repressive climate of tsarism.

Lenin was practically bald, with a small reddish goatee and sharp piercing eyes. At the core of Lenin's personality was an unquestioning belief in himself. He was absolutely certain that his political beliefs would be proven correct, and he exhibited great zeal in pursuing controversies, no matter how large or small. The rejection of any of his viewpoints on theoretical, tactical, or organizational issues was often grounds for a divisive break with former comrades. Lenin could be vicious in debate and unsparing in his criticism of party comrades and foes alike. Yet, he remained an incomparable political leader, a towering intellect, and the dominant personality among the Russian revolutionaries.

Lenin served as the head of the Soviet government and the Bolshevik party from the October Revolution through the Civil War, but his active role in Soviet political life after 1921 was hindered by his faltering health. From 1922 to 1923, Lenin was struck down by a series of strokes that left him paralyzed and barely able to speak. In the last years of his life, Lenin began to realize that the Revolution had become horribly trapped in a stultifying bureaucracy; he wrote several articles calling for political reform and sought to remove Joseph Stalin as general secretary of the party. However, his illness was too serious to allow him to agitate for his views and he died in January, 1924 before any significant changes could be made.

Following the writings of Karl Marx, a German philosopher and revolutionary, Russian Marxists repudiated the Populists' terrorist tactics and their one-sided fascination with the peasantry. They believed capitalism was inevitable in Russia and saw the working class (also known as the proletariat), whom Marx believed "had nothing to lose but its chains," as the natural constituency of a revolutionary movement. Although numerically small, the Russian proletariat would eventually develop a consciousness of its class interests and political strength and would form the core of a new revolutionary party.

These revolutionaries, variously referred to as socialists, communists, or social democrats, believed they also offered a unique "scientific" theory of history that provided the key analysis of Russia's destiny. All societies, the social democrats maintained, passed through similar stages of historical development. Feudal societies, as exemplified by tsarist Russia, would inevitably be transcended by a revolution, led by the middle classes (bourgeoisie), that instituted a constitutional democracy and laid the foundations for greater economic progress. Over time, the working class would grow to become the largest social group in society, but it would also become even more dehumanized, exploited, and impoverished under capitalism. These conditions would eventually spark another revolution, this time directed by the working class, that would replace capitalism with a socialist society. A more advanced stage of socialism, known as communism, then would emerge to abolish classes and private property and create a society based on Marx's famous slogan "From each according to his abilities, to each according to his needs."

A revolution leading to socialism was the dream of every Russian social democrat, yet no one could predict with absolute certainty how long a time period had to elapse before one historical stage followed another. Indeed, the method, timing, and details of the process, especially as regards the duration between the bourgeois and socialist revolutions, sparked endless debates among the Russian social democrats and would assume dramatic importance in the development of the 1917 revolution.

There were two primary political groupings within Russian Marxism. The first, the Socialist Revolutionaries (SRs), was founded in 1901 and represented a unique blend of Populist and Marxist ideology. The SRs accepted the revolutionary role of the working class yet envisioned an agrarian socialist society in which the Russian peasants would dominate. Indeed, their primary base of support was among the peasantry, which enthusiastically endorsed the SRs' promise of radical land reform that would transfer all land to those who worked it. Unlike other Marxist groups however, the SRs also embraced the political terror of their Populist predecessors; in the early part of the century, they carried out hundreds of assassinations against tsarist officials. Two members of the party, Alexander Kerensky and Viktor Chernov, were destined to play key roles in the events of 1917.

The second grouping within Russian Marxism was the Russian Social Democratic Labor Party (RSDLP), which emerged in the late 1890s. The party was led by veterans of the revolutionary struggle who had been won over to the side of social democracy: Georgy Plekhanov, Julius Martov, Vera Zasulich, Pavel Axelrod, as well as the 30-year-old Vladimir Lenin, who had joined the party after his release from confinement in exile in 1900. At the second Congress of the RSDLP in July 1903, a seemingly trivial difference among party members escalated into a divisive confrontation that led to an irreconcilable split within the party's ranks.

The dispute outwardly involved changes in a minor paragraph of the party statutes, but essentially it concerned the makeup of the revolutionary party itself. There were two competing views at the Congress that implied two competing conceptions of a revolutionary organization. Lenin wanted to restrict party membership to a small circle of active, full-time revolutionaries, linked in a highly disciplined, ideologically unified, and centralized apparatus. Martov envisaged the party as a looser association, embracing both professional revolutionaries and those among the working and middle classes who sympathized with the party's political program yet only contributed on a part-time basis.

No one in the revolutionary movement anticipated that these minor differences would be enough to cause a major break, but the participants became embroiled in intense personal differences as well. Comrades were transformed into mortal enemies overnight and minor arguments magnified into malicious suspicion. Both sides fervently rationalized the dispute as a deeper, more fundamental difference of political principles and maintained that there was an unbridgeable gap between them. After a long and bitter debate, Lenin's position carried by a majority of two. His followers were subsequently labeled Bolsheviks (people of the majority) and Martov's supporters became known as Mensheviks (the minority). In the following years, the two factions eventually evolved into separate political parties with clearcut political identities. They often seemed to devote as much time to damning each other as they did to struggling against tsarism, but this infighting was temporarily suspended in the fateful events of 1905.

THE REVOLUTION OF 1905

Until 1905, revolutionary struggles against tsarism were primarily an affair of small groups and courageous individuals. But in this critical year, the Russian masses were finally stirred into action on a large scale. The flashpoint was triggered in January 1904 when Russia became embroiled in a futile war in the Far East that was marked by one disaster and humiliation after another. In January 1905, the Japanese destroyed the major part of the Russian fleet in a surprise attack on Port Arthur. Further reinforcements were annihilated in the Battle of Tsushima in May. The peace treaty signed shortly after this debacle forced Russia to cede large portions of its territory to the victorious Japanese. Each defeat severely dampened the patriotic enthusiasm of the population and lowered the prestige of the government in the eyes of the masses.

On Sunday, January 22, 1905, the workers of St. Petersburg, along with their wives and children, led by Father Gapon, a former prison chaplain, marched in an enormous procession to the Winter Palace. Singing religious and patriotic songs and holding aloft holy icons, church banners, and the tsar's portrait, they appealed to the tsar to alleviate their misery and redress their grievances. "We are impoverished and oppressed, unbearable work is imposed on us, we are despised and not recognized as human beings" read the protestors' petition. "We are treated as slaves, who must bear their fate and be silent. We have suffered terrible things but we are pressed ever deeper into the abyss of poverty, ignorance and lack of rights." The marchers found the gates of the palace blocked by police and army regiments and their requests to speak with the tsar were dismissed. Without warning, the day suddenly exploded with an ominous thunder. A murderous volley was fired into the crowd by the army, leaving 800 dead and wounded and staining the snow scarlet with the blood of the protestors. Bloody Sunday, as the incident became known, shattered forever the idyllic image of the tsar and opened the floodgates to an explosion of protest.

For the next 10 months, all of Russia was convulsed in a vast social upheaval that rocked the foundations of tsarism. A resurgent workers movement dramatically intensified its strike activity: struggles for an eight-hour day and decent wages became nearly universal in Russia's factories. In late October, a nationwide railroad strike grew into a general strike that virtually paralyzed the entire country. Unrest also spread to the countryside, where peasants withheld their taxes, looted and burned nobles' estates, and demanded radical changes in land-holding practices.

Workers developed an increasing sense of class consciousness and unity and a new awareness that they could solve their own problems. At the height of the October insurgency, the workers of St. Petersburg formed the Soviet (which means "council" in Russian) of Workers' Deputies. This historic body began as a strike committee, with members drawn from factories and the revolutionary parties, but within a short time it grew into the first popularly elected legislature in Russian history. One delegate was chosen for every 500 workers in the city, and each revolutionary party sought to have its activists represented in the assembly. In its 50-day existence, the St. Petersburg Soviet gained extraordinary prestige among the working class of the city and of the nation. It became a vivid testament to the energy and creativity of the previously powerless workers. The Soviet was a beehive of activity, providing emergency municipal services during the general strike, debating political manifestos and resolutions, publishing a daily newspaper, and leading the fight for better working conditions and workers' rights in the factories. The president of its executive committee was the 26-year-old Menshevik Leon Trotsky, who would attain even greater fame in the 1917 Revolution.

The massive protest of the working classes enjoyed the active support and sympathy of elite circles as well. Upper-class reformers, who had previously recoiled from any outright display of disloyalty to the regime, now felt sufficiently emboldened to call for the immediate meeting of a constituent assembly (a popularly elected legislature). They astutely recognized that the vast scale of militancy created a radically different political situation in which reforms could be gained.

For decades the autocracy had resisted the clamor for reform raised by the intelligentsia and more enlightened sections of the bureaucracy. It responded to every outburst of popular dissent with sterner measures and increased police brutality.

With the present upheaval in the cities and the countryside, the tsar's hands were tied: he could no longer risk a policy of terror and was hence increasingly vulnerable to pressure for reform. With the autocracy under tremendous pressure in October from the general strike sweeping Russia, Nicholas II issued his October manifesto that conceded the need for a constitution, civil liberties, and a democratically mandated legislature. It was widely and enthusiastically heralded as the beginning of a new era, a first step toward the establishment of a constitutional monarchy and a parliamentary democracy. Yet the promise of democracy was dashed. The newly elected Duma (legislature) was a weak institution with no control over the decisions of government ministers. Soon after its inception the Duma passed a nearly unanimous vote of no confidence in the tsarist government, but it had absolutely no effect. Ministers continued to be responsible only to the tsar, and he ruled the country without the slightest concession to the elected assembly.

The October manifesto marked the turning of the tide back in favor of the autocracy. Enough liberal opponents threw their support to the paltry reforms to enable the tsar to give free rein to the police to crush the popular revolution once and for all. General Trepov, minister of the interior, ordered the police to "spare no bullets" in their suppression of the masses. In December, with the St. Petersburg Soviet on the verge of calling for another general strike, the entire executive committee of the soviet was imprisoned. An armed insurrection in Moscow was brutally crushed, and the army was sent to rural areas to enforce martial law. Every peasant was treated as a potential enemy: villagers were executed at random and their homes and farms burned. By early 1906 every last vestige of the "year of revolution" had been wiped away by the tsarist reaction.

THE AFTERMATH OF 1905

The autocracy was shaken to its very core, yet it emerged from the abyss of revolution relatively unscathed. Its police regime remained as pervasive and all powerful as ever, civil liberties were routinely suspended for the bulk of the population, and new legislation that promised equal treatment under the law was in effect circumvented. Trade unions were legalized on paper but were regularly closed down by the police. All political parties, including the social democrats, were permitted to run candidates for Duma elections, yet their individual members were liable to arrest. Socialist activists were fired from their work place, their newspapers were suppressed, and most social democratic leaders were compelled to emigrate in order to escape imprisonment and exile.

Although the framework of democracy that had been won in 1905 stayed in place, the tsar frustrated every attempt to infuse the legislative institutions with a life of their own. The First and Second Dumas of 1906–07 lacked even minimal independence and represented no real challenge to the autocracy. All legislation passed by the Duma required the approval of the tsar to become law. Nicholas also retained the right to pass any decree he saw fit when the parliament was not in session. Even with these handicaps the Duma proved to be too insubordinate for the tsar: a mere 72 days after the first Duma convened, the tsar sent troops to close it down, and the second Duma was likewise dissolved in short fashion. Elections for subsequent Dumas were based on an electoral formula that virtually eliminated all but the wealthiest Russians from voting. The experiment with democracy died a quick, unhappy death.

Tsarist Russia may have survived the Revolution of 1905, but the momentous events of that year cast a long shadow over future developments. The tsar's strategic retreat and minimal reforms successfully preserved the autocracy but they did nothing to resolve the fundamental contradictions of Russian society. The peasants' desperate land hunger had gone unfulfilled, the workers' pleas for a decent life had gone unanswered, and the democratic aspirations of the liberal reformers, indeed of the entire society, had gone unmet. It appeared likely that there might be a renewed confrontation with these same social forces in the near future.

CHAPTER TWO NOTES

p. 17   "There is no better way . . ." Alexander Ulyanov, quoted in Liebman, p. 52.

p. 22   "We are impoverished and oppressed . . ." Chamberlin, William.
        The Russian Revolution, 1917–1921 (New York: Macmillan, 1935),
        p. 48.

CHAPTER 3

THE GREAT WAR

On July 17, 1914, the Archduke Francis Ferdinand, heir to the throne of Emperor Francis Joseph of Austria-Hungary, and his wife were visiting Sarajevo, the capital of Bosnia, on their wedding anniversary. As they were reviewing a regiment of troops that had been mustered in their honor, a young Serbian nationalist leaped out of the onlooking crowd and fired at the open carriage, killing the archduke and his wife. These shots echoed around the world. Within weeks, all of Europe was plunged into the abyss of the Great War, later famous as World War I. When it reached its end four years later, 35 million people had been killed or wounded in the conflict. A generation of young Europeans vanished forever, the political map of the continent was irrevocably altered, and revolution left its fateful imprint on Russian history.

Before 1914, two generations of Europeans had grown up without the shadow of war. For more than four decades, Europe enjoyed a tranquil peace, marked by dazzling technological discoveries, an unprecedented rise in living standards, stunning new cultural accomplishments, and the progressive extension of democracy throughout the continent. Yet this stability was built on quicksand. All of the great powers of Europe were linked in a rigid system of military alliances, based on a universal faith in preserving a balance of power among them. Each country sought to maintain its power and interests against all possible adversaries, and through the use of secret treaties and protocols, enlisted the help of allied nations who pledged to come to its aid in case of a conflict.

This framework collapsed in 1914 amid a series of miscalculations, bluffs, and counterthreats as each country drew to the brink of war and back. The assassination of Ferdinand set the chain of events in motion. Austria-Hungary, which was aligned with Germany, had annexed the region of Bosnia years earlier, angering the Serbs, who considered Bosnia to be part of Serbian territory. Using the murder as a pretext and determined to humiliate Serbia, Austria-Hungary issued an ultimatum that demanded a formal apology and territorial concessions from Serbia. However, Russia, which was allied with Serbia, also had interests in the Balkans. It warned Austria that it would stand by its ally in case of attack. Russia was supported by France and Great Britain, whose main objective was to keep Germany's ambitions in check.

On July 28, Austria ignored Russia's warning and declared war on Serbia; the next day, Austrian troops were sent on the attack. On July 30, Russia ordered the mobilization of its forces in response to Austria's offensive. This provoked a stern admonition the following day from Germany, Austria's ally, which demanded that Russia halt any further troop movements and that France promise to remain neutral in the event of a war between Russia and Germany. Both Russia and France ignored these demands, so on August 1, Germany declared war on Russia. Russia responded in kind the next day, followed shortly by France and Great Britain. A war that no one had wanted came about because Europe's leaders saw fit to gamble the lives of their populations in a grandiose game of "chicken."

RUSSIA ENTERS THE WAR

Russia in 1914 had good reasons to avoid war. Its economy was not equipped to fight a prolonged war under modern conditions. Its food production and railway system were totally antiquated. There were no pressing territorial claims involved in the conflict, nor was there any direct threat to Russia's territorial integrity. The social climate was even less favorable for such a war. Only a decade earlier, the regime had barely survived a major conflict with Japan and the tensions of 1905 had by no means been alleviated. "A general European war is mortally dangerous for both Russia and Germany no matter who wins," warned the reactionary Peter Durnovo in a prophetic memorandum to the tsar in early 1914. "There must inevitably break out in the defeated country a social revolution which, by the very nature of things, will spread to the country of the victor."

Why Russia chose war under these unfavorable circumstances cannot be explained as merely loyalty to its diplomatic commitments but rather needs to be looked at in terms of the tsarist regime itself. The humiliation of defeat in 1905 created widespread frustration, leading to a resurgent nationalism that infected Russia's ruling elites. Duma liberals and conservatives alike demanded that Russia regain its lost glory and assert its rightful control over its sphere of interest in the Balkans. The autocracy's urgent need to recoup its former prestige demanded a popular war that could unite the entire population around the tsar. Naked self-interest was involved as well. Russia's victory in the war, as provided in the secret agreements between the Allies, would assure its control over the Turkish port of Constantinople and the Dardanelles, which would in turn safeguard Russia's international commerce from all foreign interference.

The war was also the result of foolish miscalculation. After 40 years of peace, "all imagined that it would be an affair of great marches and great battles, quickly decided," wrote historian A. J. P. Taylor. "It would all be over by Christmas." No one could possibly have imagined the suffering that would result, but even after the tragedy of the unrelenting slaughter had become obvious to everyone, the war was stubbornly pursued by the tsar and the other European leaders. Ultimately, the Great War was a great folly for all the conservative monarchies of Europe; by its end, every monarchy save Great Britain would pass into history. By placing such enormous demands on Russian society at a time when so many fundamental problems remained unresolved, the war sounded the death knell for any chance of peaceful reform and also for tsarism as well.

On the evening of August 2, 1914, the tsar announced Russia's entry into the war. His proclamation generated an outburst of patriotic enthusiasm on an unprecedented scale. In the first days of the war, the streets of Russia's cities were packed with marches, parades, and demonstrations in favor of Russia's mission. St. Petersburg, thought by the public to be a German sounding name, was renamed Petrograd, in a wave of anti-German fervor. Liberal opponents of the regime agreed to postpone their struggle for political and social reforms until after the war had been brought to a successful conclusion.

The outbreak of the war, however, confronted Russian socialists, along with their European counterparts, with the stark choice between loyalty to their country or allegiance to the principles of international socialism. European socialist parties, loosely affiliated in an alliance known as the Second International, had always strongly espoused a commitment to peace, pacifism, and a strict policy of noninterference in the national affairs of other countries. Socialists emphasized the fraternity of the working classes across national boundaries; every worker should resist fighting in any war that asked one worker to kill another on behalf of the "fatherland."

Yet as soon as war was declared, the leaders of the European socialist parties hastily abandoned all their solemn antiwar vows and called upon their followers to defend their respective countries. In a stunning betrayal of their most cherished principles, the leaders of the social democrats in Austria, Belgium, France, Germany, and Great Britain, voted to approve money for the war in their legislatures. In many cases, socialists accepted ministerial positions in wartime cabinets. "It became quite difficult to distinguish," wrote historian Marcel Liebman, "between the former champions of peace and universal brotherhood and those whose warmongering they had always denounced."

Although the Russian socialists abstained in the Duma vote on war funding, the war proved to be a bitterly divisive issue for them as well. Generally, within each of the socialist parties, there emerged "defensist" factions, who openly endorsed the war, and "internationalist" factions, who called for an immediate peace with neither victors nor vanquished. Defensism was considerably stronger among the Mensheviks and Socialist Revolutionaries than among the Bolsheviks. Prominent leaders of these two parties rallied to the war cause, and like the Russian liberals, called for a postponement of the struggle against the tsar until the Germans were defeated. The Internationalists, represented by Julius Martov of the Mensheviks, Viktor Chernov of the Socialist Revolutionaries, and virtually all of the Bolshevik leadership, saw the triumph of either the Central Powers (Germany, Austria-Hungary) or the Allies (Great Britain, France, Russia) as equally damaging to the cause of socialism. They condemned the war policy advocated by other socialists and called for an immediate peace between all belligerent nations. This division within the socialist ranks was to have profound consequences for the outcome of the Revolution.

RUSSIA AT WAR

The mass slaughter of World War I commenced in early August 1914 with the Russian offensive against the German forces in East Prussia. Two Russian armies swept forward, enjoying a brief though illusory moment of success while the Germans were momentarily preoccupied on the Western Front. Within two weeks, however, the Germans halted the advance, and after two experienced generals were appointed to command their eastern forces, the Germans counterattacked and achieved a resounding victory in the Battle of Tannenberg. As chronicled by Alexander Solzhenitsyn in his evocative account *August 1914*, the Germans first lured one of the Russian armies into an ingenious trap, capturing the entire force in a daring encirclement, and then wheeled on the flank of the other army and utterly destroyed it. Three hundred thousand soldiers were captured, wounded, or killed in this single battle.

By the end of 1914, the Russian army had suffered another 500,000 casualties, almost half of whom were killed in action. Nearly one-half of Russia's prewar manpower was expended in just six months. In the fall, Russia scored a series of victories against the Austrians in the southeast, but in the spring of 1915, the Germans and Austrians launched a withering offensive all along the Eastern Front. Over the next five months, the Russian armies endured constant retreat and rearguard fighting. Their lines were driven back 500 miles, forcing them to abandon Galicia, Poland, and most of White Russia. The Russian casualties were staggering: close to one million dead and wounded with almost another million lost as prisoners of war. Then, over the next two years, the German and Russian positions settled into a self-destructive stalemate and the major action of the war shifted to the Western Front.

The explanation for this immense debacle was rooted in the fundamental inadequacies of the tsarist system. World War I was the first modern war in which the entire industrial resources of a nation were mobilized. New weapons of advanced technology (the tank, airplane, and poison gas), the outfitting of millions of men over a prolonged period, the rapid movement and coordination of troops and equipment

SOLZHENITSYN AND THE TURNING POINT OF AUGUST 1914

Alexander Solzhenitsyn is one of the foremost Russian novelists of the 20th century. He was awarded the Nobel Prize in Literature in 1971 for his remarkable novels depicting life in Stalinist Russia: *One Day in the Life of Ivan Denisovich*, *First Circle*, and *Cancer Ward*. Solzhenitsyn was deported from the Soviet Union in 1974 after the publication of *The Gulag Archipelago*, an unsparing account of the vast Soviet prison system, but he made a triumphant return to his native land in May 1994 after 20 years of exile in the United States.

While in exile, Solzhenitsyn completed a massive 10-volume fictional epic of the revolutionary era, entitled *The Red Wheel*. The first novel in the series, *August 1914*, is a powerful portrait of the terrible defeat of the Russian Second Army at the Battle of Tannenberg at the start of World War I. The novel's epic scope, sweeping range, multitude of characters, and literary experimentation made comparisons with Leo Tolstoy's *War and Peace* inevitable. The similarity was especially apparent in both authors' focus on the central role of history. Tolstoy believed that the forces of history were unknowable and inevitable: people were powerless to change the course of history, which he felt was preordained. Neither of the two major figures in *War and Peace* —Napoleon, the emperor of France, nor General Kutuzov, the architect of imperial Russia's triumph against the French army—could make any difference in the outcome of the battles that they thought they were directing.

In *August 1914*, Solzhenitsyn is intent on refuting Tolstoy's argument and wants to reassert the importance of the individual in history. He offers a vivid depiction of the idiotic bungling of the Russian general staff: the neglect of elementary details over vast spaces—each of these required the combatant nations to harness its economic strength and to adjust quickly to changing circumstances. Russia, in this regard, was operating at a major disadvantage.

of supply and transport so that troops march for five days along a railway when they might have been sent by train; orders for retreat being given in the midst of a winning skirmish; the refusal to commit needed reinforcements at a key time in a battle; the careless transmittal of uncoded radio messages that allows the Germans to be informed of Russian troop movements. Yet despite the weakness and inefficiency of the military system, a single individual can still make a difference. After the ineptness of a Russian general has left thousands of Russian troops stranded behind enemy lines, the hero of Solzhenitsyn's novel, Colonel Vorotyntsev, rallies the Russian forces through his own bravery and leadership. His initiative gives the Second Army a chance to launch a devastating counterblow against the Germans, but the opportunity is not seized because of the incompetence of the high command.

History for Solzhenitsyn is never fixed but always contingent: there are critical moments in history, which he calls "knots," when more favorable alternatives can be achieved or irrevocably lost depending on the course of human intervention. 1914, for Solzhenitsyn, was not merely a disastrous episode in a long and disastrous war but the turning point in modern Russian history. The catastrophe at Tannenberg in August 1914, he maintains, obliterated all other possibilities for peaceful development and paved the way for the revolutions of 1917. Of course, even if one acknowledges the force of Solzhenitsyn's argument, it does not automatically follow that if Russia's leadership and preparations had been sufficient to avert defeat in August 1914, the contradictions that led to revolution would necessarily have been peacefully resolved. The crisis of the tsarist system was not merely a matter of individual failures but rather the cumulative impact of the collapse of Russia's economic, social, and political structures, and it remains hard to see how the Revolutionary downfall of tsarism could have been averted.

It was fighting a 20th-century war with a 19th-century government and society.

Russia entered the war with a million fewer rifles in its arsenals than the number of men mobilized into its army. It suffered extraordinary shortages of ammunition, weapons, boots, uniforms, and food. It could field only 60 batteries of heavy artillery against the Germans' nearly 400, and none of the Russian guns were the Germans' equal in either range or caliber. Its rail system collapsed under the terrible strain of heavy military demands and expanded domestic production. None of these inadequacies were corrected by the incompetent and corrupt tsarist regime.

The devastating losses were also the product of a military leadership whose incompetence and insensitivity were staggering. Russian generals callously chose to compensate for the shortages of weapons and supplies with their seemingly inexhaustible supply of manpower: entire divisions and regiments were decimated in single battles; others suffered an endless attrition that reduced them to a mere fraction of their original strength. They persisted in large frontal assaults against impregnable defensive positions long after the futility of such a strategy became obvious to even the most inexperienced soldier. Hundreds of thousands of lives were sacrificed in waves of suicidal attacks against the German lines. There was rarely any real prize to be captured or essential tactical position worth attaining, only the arrogance of officers willing to squander the lives of their own men for a brief taste of glory.

The experience of war left millions of soldiers crippled and scarred with deep wounds of both body and spirit. Every soldier was aware of his superior's ineptitude and could see how easily the Russian armies were outmaneuvered by the Germans. Soldiers began to distrust their officers, who seemed so quick to send them to their senseless deaths in the name of the tsar. "They are ready to fight to the last drop of my blood," complained one soldier. A pervasive war weariness and demoralization spread through the ranks. Every soldier doubted that the carnage would ever end or that anything even remotely resembling victory would ever be achieved. Every peasant recruit, who made up the bulk of the Russian army, longed for nothing more than to return to his village alive and in one piece. "Everyone to the last man was interested in nothing but peace," wrote one soldier. "Who should win and what kind of peace it would be, that was of small interest to the army. It wanted peace at any cost, for it was weary of war."

It was inevitable that such prolonged bloodshed would lead to increased criticism and questions about the government and the tsar. One soldier concluded: "A fish begins to stink from the head. What kind of tsar is it who surrounds himself with thieves and chisellers? It is as clear as day that we're going to lose the war."

THE DISINTEGRATION OF THE AUTOCRACY

This young soldier was not the only one to notice that the monarchy was careening madly out of control. Indeed the last three years of the regime were characterized by an endless litany of mistakes and misjudgments. The first of these was Nicholas's disastrous decision in the fall of 1915 to assume personal control of the Russian army, without any consultation and over the objections of his ministers and advisers. The tsar had no experience of command and no claim to tactical or strategic insight. He was no more equipped to be commander in chief than he was to be the leader of the nation.

With the tsar preoccupied with military affairs in army headquarters outside Petrograd, the tsarina became his chief deputy with virtual control over the country's domestic affairs. Alexandra was even more unsuited for leadership than her husband was. She possessed extreme reactionary political views and a paranoid disposition that grew worse as the pressures of governance undermined her physical and mental health. The tsarina imagined herself surrounded by a host of enemies, broadly considered to include everyone and anyone who spoke ill of the regime, whom she believed were conspiring to betray her and her husband. Alexandra surrounded herself with a group of fawning advisers, spiritualists who claimed to speak with the dead, charlatans promising homemade cures, and swindlers and adventurers of all kinds. Her closest confidant and spiritual adviser was a man who combined all of these faults—Gregory Rasputin. Rasputin was an illiterate peasant and fraudulent mystic, whose hold over the royal family came from his mysterious ability to alleviate the suffering of the royal heir, Alexei, who was afflicted with hemophilia. Alexandra was convinced that Rasputin had been sent by God to heal her son's bleeding disease, and she had unquestioning faith in his judgment. She refused to give any credence to the flood of reports about Rasputin's sexual escapades, notorious debaucheries, and innumerable public indiscretions, gossip of which widely circulated in the capital.

Rasputin's influence with the tsarina became a matter of urgent public concern when it became obvious that he enjoyed substantial input into public policy. He and Alexandra bombarded Nicholas with such a meddlesome stream of advice, requests, and demands that the tsar complained: "Sometimes it seems that it is not so much he who helps me govern my country, as I who helps him run the government." Government ministers were required to submit their policies for Rasputin's approval, and he named his own puppets to virtually every government post. Rasputin and Alexandra replaced ministers with a bewildering frequency; able statespeople were supplanted by a motley assortment of rogues, nonentities, and incompetents. "Disorganization has become such," said one critic, "that we might believe ourselves to be in a lunatic asylum."

The political disintegration of tsarism was made even worse in light of the menacing economic crisis that threatened Russia. The war made all of the structural weaknesses of the Russian economy worse. The railroad system was on the brink of collapse due to the extra demands of the war, and this transport crisis led in turn to severe bottlenecks throughout every branch of industry. Industrial firms were forced to cut back production because of irregular fuel deliveries; this led to shortages of consumer goods and rising unemployment. Peasants refused to produce sufficient grain for the cities because there were hardly any manufactured goods that they could purchase. The resulting shortages of food and essential items drove prices sky high, triggering serious inflation. Fewer and fewer Russians could afford the basic necessities of life, such as sufficient coal or wood to keep their homes above the freezing point. By the winter of 1916, the Russian people had reached the breaking point, and bitterness and dissent were widespread and open.

Dissatisfaction with the autocracy spread to the upper reaches of Russian political life as well. Once the staggering incompetence of the government became widely known, not only the old political opposition but also the conservative Duma deputies who had numbered among the regime's most adamant supporters were driven to open hostility.

In a devastating indictment of tsarism in the Duma chambers, the leader of the liberal party Constitutional Democrats (Kadets), Paul Miliukov, issued a series of stinging attacks against government policies, concluding each charge with the phrase: "Is this stupidity or is this treason?" Aristocrats, conservatives, and liberals alike begged Nicholas to grant some kind of dramatic concession to placate public opinion.

Rumors surfaced about palace intrigues to force the tsar to abdicate or plans by conservatives or liberals to foment a coup d'etat that would replace Nicholas with a government of Duma deputies. But the plots came to nothing. The only conspiracy that was successfully carried out, albeit with a touch of black comedy, was the assassination of Rasputin by two leading members of the aristocracy. They lured Rasputin to a prearranged rendezvous where they tainted his food and drink with cyanide. Unfortunately for the conspirators, the poison did not appear to produce any ill effect on the mystic, who continued to imbibe with his customary vigor. One of the conspirators then shot him several times point blank and watched in horror as the wounded Rasputin rose to his feet and stumbled out of the apartment. The assassins chased him into the winter night and, after repeated near misses, finally shot Rasputin dead. They attempted to hide all evidence of the crime by dropping his body into the Neva River, but heavy ice flows kept the body afloat and the murder was discovered the next day. The deed was greeted with broad public sympathy, and Rasputin's bumbling murderers were merely exiled to their country estates for the crime. Rasputin's assassins hoped that by ridding the regime of the man who symbolized its decadence, they might yet save it, but the assassination changed nothing. Both the tsar and tsarina refused every concession, dismissed every offer of compromise, and stayed resolute in their insistence on retaining absolute power.

As the new year of 1917 dawned, signs of the impending crisis grew acute. A desperate food crisis gripped Petrograd as the city's daily bread supplies dropped to a fraction of its requirements. After years of wartime quiet, there was a dramatic revival of strikes that winter and revolutionaries began to recruit new adherents to their cause among the ranks of the dissatisfied workers. Still, the tsar considered his position to be unassailable. He could continue to rely on the 180,000-strong Petrograd garrison and the police corps to enforce his will and

„Хлеба"

С картины художн. Соколова-Скаля

VI—26

"Bread!" All segments of Russian society—the workers, soldiers, and peasants—united against the tsarist regime. (Library of Congress)

crush any revolutionary uprising. However, the garrison, originally composed of elite troops, had suffered grievous losses in the early phases of the war and now was composed almost entirely of raw, undisciplined recruits from the countryside. Many of these new soldiers shared the immense discontent of the rest of the population and were not enthusiastic at all about being sent to the front. There was some question about what their behavior would be if faced with the task of repressing the masses, yet the tsarist authorities assumed that their loyalty was unshakeable.

Their optimism was equally matched by the pessimism of the Russian revolutionaries abroad. Most of the social democratic leaders spent the war years in exile in neutral countries, isolated and out of touch with events in their homeland. When they surveyed the bloody wreckage scattered on the battlefields of Europe, with the knowledge that their former socialist colleagues had contributed to the slaughter, many wondered if they were not now swimming against the tide of history. Many questioned whether they would ever see a revolution in their lifetimes. "We of the older generation," Lenin told an audience of students in January 1917, "may not live to see the decisive battles of the coming revolution." Within a month though, a new world would dawn for Russia and the world.

CHAPTER THREE NOTES

p. 28   "A general European war is mortally . . ." Peter Durnovo, quoted in Bruce Lincoln. *The Romanovs* (New York: Simon and Schuster, 1981), p. 683.

p. 30   "It became quite difficult to distinguish . . ." Liebman, p. 93

p. 34   "They are ready to fight . . ." Quoted in Allan Wildman. *The End of the Imperial Army* (Princeton: Princeton University Press, 1980), p. 108.

p. 35   "A fish begins to stink . . ." Wildman, p. 92

p. 36   "Sometimes it seems that . . ." Tsar Nicholas II, quoted in Liebman, p. 80.

p. 36   "Disorganization has become such . . ." Liebman, p. 77.

p. 37   "Is this stupidity . . ." Chamberlan, p. 69.

p. 39   "We of the older generation . . ." Vladimir Lenin, quoted in Christopher Rice. *Lenin: A Portrait of a Professional Rebel* (London: Cassell Publishers, 1990), p. 135.

CHAPTER 4

THE FEBRUARY REVOLUTION

While even the most revolutionary of men despaired, it was the women of Petrograd who struck the spark that ignited the Russian Revolution. Thursday, February 23, 1917 was to be celebrated by socialist groups as International Women's Day and would feature a protest march by women workers. No one had the slightest intimation that this might be the first day of the Revolution. Most socialists had only halfheartedly promoted the occasion. Only a small number of propaganda leaflets had been distributed. Not a single organization had urged the other Petrograd workers to strike in support of the women's demonstration. Most revolutionaries felt the time was not ripe for militant action.

However, as historian Tsuygoshi Hasegawa writes in *The February Revolution: Petrograd 1917*:

> The revolutionaries underestimated the despair and rage of the female workers. After their husbands and sons had gone to the front, all the burden of supporting families fell upon them. They worked from dawn to dusk, sometimes for as long as thirteen hours, to earn low wages that could not catch up with ever increasing prices and after the long day they stood in long lines

in the freezing cold just to get a loaf of bread. No propaganda was necessary to incite these women to action.

The day before, incensed housewives, driven by hunger and frustration, had invaded bakeries and other food shops. The city stood unknowingly on the brink of dramatic change.

THE OPENING MOMENTS

On the morning of February 23, women at the textile mills in the Vyborg district abandoned their machines and moved out into the streets, shouting over and over "Bread!" Inside other factories, male workers heard the impassioned voices of the women protestors. Many stopped working and moved to the windows, where the women implored them to join the strike. Workers at one factory after another voted to cast their lot with the demonstrators and joined the rapidly growing crowd. Processions of workers moved through the Vyborg district, drawing people from other factories in their wake.

By the early afternoon, more than 50,000 workers were on strike. The streets echoed with the workers' rousing cries of "Bread!" . . . "We Have Nothing to Eat!" . . . "Our Children Are Starving!" Seditious chants of "Down with the Autocracy" and "Stop the War" were enthusiastically echoed by the crowd. There were a few isolated clashes with the police, but no serious injuries occurred. By evening, the demonstrators had returned home and the Vyborg was quiet once again. None of the authorities appeared unduly concerned by the day's events. After a visit with his family, Nicholas II returned by train to his remote military headquarters at Mohilev, 100 miles south of the capital. Yet in the working-class districts of Petrograd, the atmosphere was electric, with workers eagerly discussing what the next day would bring.

On the next morning, February 24, there was a tremendous sense of excitement and anticipation in the workers' districts. Political rallies were held in numerous workplaces, with speakers openly denouncing the tsarist government. Socialist militants and organizers canvassed factories throughout the city, appealing to workers to join the strike movement. By nine in the morning, the streets of the Vyborg district were already packed with striking workers carrying placards aloft and shouting slogans at the top of their lungs. The strike spread to every working-class area of Petrograd, and university students joined in the protests. More than 150,000 workers and 130 factories—twice the number of the previous day—participated in the protests.

As the crowd of workers massed along the Sampsonievsky Prospekt in the Vyborg district, 500 police, including two companies of mounted Cossacks (elite calvary from the Cossack region of Russia), were sent to confront the demonstrators. After police officers on horseback charged into the crowd, the Cossacks galloped slowly behind them with their sabers unsheathed. In spite of repeated orders from the police officers, the Cossacks refused to force the crowd to disperse. The demonstrators launched into earnest conversations with the Cossacks. One woman pleaded: "We have our husbands, fathers, brothers at the front. But here we have only hunger, hard times, injustices, shame! You also have your mothers, wives, sisters and children. All we want is bread and an end to the war."

The police had cordoned off the major bridges that led from the Vyborg district to the center of the city. In the 200 years since its founding by Peter the Great, the Russian capital had been divided into sharply defined socioeconomic districts. Most factory workers lived and worked in the far outlying suburbs or in the Vyborg and Okhra districts on the right bank of the Neva River. The central sections of the city, encompassing the so-called Petersburg side on the left side of the Neva, were the domain of the upper and middle classes. Here were the glittering palaces of the royal family, the luxurious residential buildings of the aristocracy, the imposing architectural masterpieces housing the government offices, the fashionable shops along Nevsky Prospekt, the city's finest boulevard: all of which made Petrograd one of Europe's most beautiful capitals. Rarely did the populations of the two worlds of Petrograd meet, but on this fateful Friday, the artificial walls were swept away in a tidal wave of protest.

Although the police effectively blocked the entrances to the central city, they overlooked the fact that the Neva River was frozen solid because of the severe winter cold. Thousands of workers crossed the Neva on the ice and made their way into the center. Columns of demonstrators marched through the wealthy residential neighborhoods and up and down Nevsky Prospekt. Several large rallies were held at Kazan Square, with radical slogans calling for the removal of the autocracy increasingly voiced by the orators. Police and calvary detachments attempted to disperse the rallies and marches, but workers resisted, pelting them with stones and shards of ice. The last demonstrators did not leave the Nevsky Prospekt until after eight in the evening and every worker vowed to return the following day. The

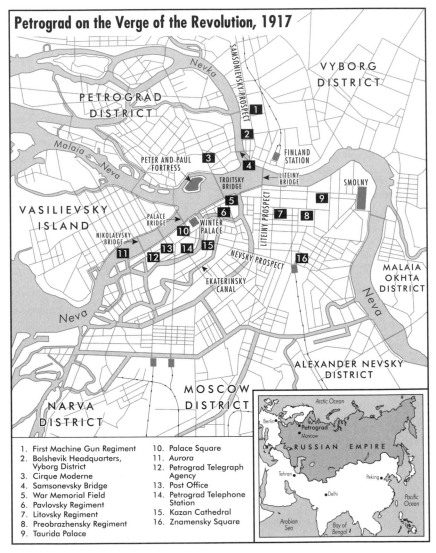

Petrograd on the Verge of the Revolution, 1917

1. First Machine Gun Regiment
2. Bolshevik Headquarters, Vyborg District
3. Cirque Moderne
4. Samsonevsky Bridge
5. War Memorial Field
6. Pavlovsky Regiment
7. Litovsky Regiment
8. Preobrazhensky Regiment
9. Taurida Palace
10. Palace Square
11. Aurora
12. Petrograd Telegraph Agency
13. Post Office
14. Petrograd Telephone Station
15. Kazan Cathedral
16. Znamensky Square

This map of Petrograd shows the major districts, streets, and bridges in which much of the action of the February Revolution took place.

past two days had convinced many that the long awaited revolution was upon them.

Yet, there was hardly any sense of urgency on the part of the tsarist government. The cabinet of ministers convened, but they did not discuss the unrest. There was no attempt to alleviate the food crisis by using the available food reserves in the city. The police had no strategy to prevent the workers from crossing the river or to isolate the workers in their own districts. The tsar made no public statement whatsoever, nor did he issue specific instructions in private to his ministers. The complacency and incompetence that had characterized the tsarist government ever since the infamous episode at Khodynka Field in 1894 remained.

THE STRUGGLE ESCALATES

By Saturday, February 25, the strike movement had escalated into a general strike that paralyzed the city and placed the government in a virtual state of siege. Trains and cabs stopped running, restaurants and hotels shut down, and no papers were published. Students, government workers, and teachers joined the demonstrations. The strike spread to every sector of the working class, including workers in small workshops, bank clerks, waiters, hotel porters, and post office employees, all of whom had little previous strike experiences. Petrograd's working-class districts were transformed into a surging sea of protestors and workers once again congregated in the city center. Thousands upon thousands marched down Nevsky Prospekt, singing revolutionary songs and holding red banners and placards.

On this third day, the momentum of the revolutionary uprising seemed irresistible, but everything still depended on the reaction of the authorities. The police, who were called the "Pharaohs" by the workers, were absolutely loyal to the tsar and would not waver in their support of the regime. The position of the Cossack regiments and the army was much more ambiguous. The workers tried to avoid any hostile encounters with both groups and hoped to win them over to the Revolution. During a huge rally at Znamensky Square, mounted police drove in and chased away demonstrators. One worker approached the Cossacks and said: "Brothers, Cossacks, help the workers in their struggle for peaceable demands. You see how the Pharaohs treat us hungry workers. Help us!" The Cossacks lowered their guns and sabers and attacked the police. When the melee finally cleared, the police officer who had mounted the first charge lay dead in the streets. Knowledge of the Cossacks' actions spread like wildfire through the city and had a dramatic effect on the street crowds.

The attitude of the army was also an open question. The bulk of the Petrograd garrison was composed largely of peasant recruits who had been temporarily exempted from serving at the front. These soldiers knew that they could end up in the bloody trenches of a war that seemed hopelessly lost. They wanted to return to their homes, their farms, and their loved ones. They had no quarrel with the Petrograd workers and even sympathized with their calls for an end to the war and relief from impoverishment. Yet, a soldier who disobeyed an officer's order to attack the workers risked losing his own life in front of a firing squad. Still, as the confrontation intensified, it had become more and more difficult for the soldiers to maintain their neutrality. At some point, they would have to make a fateful choice between conscience or obedience.

By the end of the third day, no one could doubt the gravity of the situation. It was clear that something more than simply strikes or street demonstrations was in the making. The government arrested several hundred militant workers and seized members of the Petrograd Bolshevik Committee. It also issued a proclamation ordering workers to return to their factories and warned that any demonstrator would be arrested and sent to the front. This was the first day that the Petrograd authorities considered the situation serious enough to report to the tsar, who that evening sent a telegram to General Khabalov, the commander of the Petrograd region: "I command you to suppress from tomorrow all disorders in the streets of the capital." The police and army were given permission to fire upon demonstrators should they fail to disperse.

ON THE VERGE OF REVOLUTION
Sunday, February 26 was the turning point. The streets of Petrograd became an armed camp. Soldiers and police were deployed in unprecedented numbers throughout the capital to prevent crowds from forming in the center. Nevertheless, demonstrators managed to make their way into the center of the city. As the crowds massed along Nevsky

Prospekt, they found themselves hemmed in by a picket line of soldiers deployed across the broad avenue. Without warning, the soldiers ruthlessly opened fire on the protestors. People ran for their lives, hiding in doorways or behind street lamps. Others threw themselves flat on the ground. When the smoke cleared, the dead and wounded lay scattered in the street and dark blood stains seeped onto the light covering of snow. There were three additional shooting incidents by the army that afternoon. All told, more than 300 protestors were killed or wounded. All of the troops involved in the shooting belonged to training detachments, elite military units that were used to train non-commissioned officers. By five in the evening, the hopelessness of the situation had convinced most protestors to return to their homes.

That same day, Prince Golitsyn issued a previously signed imperial decree, undated in case the need for it arose, that abruptly disbanded the Duma. The meaning of this act was perfectly clear: the autocracy was refusing to make the slightest concession to the protestors or even to its liberal supporters who were urging some sort of compromise in order to save the monarchy.

By the evening, the Revolution had reached a decisive moment, with victory or defeat hanging in the balance. While some activists were ready to call off the general strike to avert further bloodshed, the government offensive had strengthened the determination of many others to continue the struggle. Their demonstrations had grown more fervent, more determined, more courageous, as the day progressed. But now, the workers had to make a fateful choice: either withdraw and admit defeat or move forward to possible victory by way of an armed insurrection. The fate of the Revolution therefore rested entirely on the hearts and minds of the soldiers. If the troops maintained military discipline and refused to break ranks, the workers would be massacred and the tsar would emerge triumphant from this ordeal. The Revolution would be won only if the soldiers threw their full support behind the workers.

THE GREAT MUTINY

It was indeed the army that tilted the balance for the Revolution. At night, soldiers of the Pavlovsky Regiment, who had been confined to their barracks during the day, learned from workers that the regiment's training detachment had opened fire on demonstrators in front of Kazan Cathedral that afternoon. The angry soldiers, 100 strong, broke open an armory and stormed out of their barracks to restrain its training squad from further bloodshed. While they were crossing the Ekaterinsky Canal, the company spotted a group of police on the opposite bank opening fire on an unarmed crowd. As the protestors fled in horror, the soldiers of the regiment took hold of their rifles and fired—not on the demonstrators, but on the police. When they returned to their barracks, they tried to win over other companies in their regiment to the mutiny. Later that evening, however, the leaders of the revolt were imprisoned in the Fortress of Peter and Paul and General Khabalov issued a decree warning that future acts of rebellion would be punished by the death penalty. But the die had already been cast—the soldiers of Petrograd had reached the breaking point.

The next morning, February 27, an even more decisive act of rebellion occurred. The training detachment of the Volynsky Regiment had been involved in the shootings on Nevsky Prospekt on Bloody Sunday. When the soldiers returned to their barracks that evening, talk of insubordination was in the air. The soldiers debated endlessly throughout the night and reached an agreement that under no conditions would they ever carry out orders to fire on the people. When an officer arrived to read the tsar's telegram to General Khabalov in an attempt to restore order, he provoked the anger of the soldiers and was killed. Having burned their bridges behind them, the soldiers surged out onto the streets and made for the barracks of other regiments to gain new recruits. Within an hour, the Preobrazensky and Litovsky Regiments had gone over to the side of the Revolution and the armed insurrection was underway.

By noon, 25,000 soldiers had joined the mutiny. They stormed the arsenals and handed out rifles and revolvers to the Petrograd masses. Soon the city streets were filled with soldiers and workers carrying rifles with red ribbons tied around their bayonets. The soldiers crisscrossed the city in trucks, carrying red flags and machine guns, to spread the revolt. Groups of soldiers and workers stormed the prisons and released all political prisoners. The soldiers captured the building of the Petrograd Okhrana (secret police) and the Central Police headquarters. Railway stations, telegraph and telephone exchanges, and key government installations were also seized. By late afternoon, the military command was completely isolated. They had no way to contact loyalist regiments in other parts of the city and attempts at rallying troops to their defense were futile. By nightfall, almost the entire Petrograd garrison had gone over to the Revolution, and with the exception of a small area near the Admiralty Building, the entire city was controlled by the Revolutionaries.

As the insurrection progressed, events took place behind the scenes that would critically affect the course of the Revolution. There was some question of whether the Duma would disobey the tsar's order dissolving it, an act that might be perceived as positive support for the insurgents. Duma leaders met privately during the afternoon at the Tauride Palace as the turmoil progressed in the streets. Some Duma conservatives called for a military dictatorship, while liberals in the majority adopted a more pragmatic wait-and-see attitude. However, events outpaced the liberals' timidity. By late afternoon, thousands of workers and soldiers appeared at the Tauride demanding to know where the new government was. The liberals, who had shrunk from outright support for the Revolution, now had no choice but to assume

During the February Revolution, workers and soldiers burned the Romanov coat of arms. (Library of Congress)

power. They formed a Provisional Committee that evolved into the new Provisional Government.

That same day, militant workers and socialist party leaders resurrected the Petrograd Soviet (workers' council), which had first sprung up during the 1905 Revolution. Throughout the afternoon and into the

Soldiers carried banners in honor of the martyrs of February. (Library of Congress)

THE MARTYRS
OF FEBRUARY

A month after the February Revolution, on March 23, 1917, the citizens of Petrograd gathered to honor the martyrs who had lost their lives in the revolutionary protests. An endless procession of workers and soldiers, estimated at nearly one million people, paraded through the streets of the capital, carrying banners and the coffins of their fallen comrades. "In this gala procession of hundreds of thousands of people," wrote the famed writer Maxim Gorky, "it was felt, and for the first time, that the Russian people, yes the Russian people, had made a revolution. It rose from the dead to join the great cause evening, worker delegates packed into a tiny room at the Tauride Palace, where they heard a continuous stream of reports of the days events from insurgent soldiers. In the evening, a motion was passed to change the name of the Soviet of Workers to the Soviet of Workers' and Soldiers' Deputies. Henceforth, delegates from the factory and the

of the world—the building of new and ever-so-free forms of life." As the bodies of the fallen heroes were lowered to their graves in the Field of Mars outside the city, the guns of the Peter and Paul Fortress sounded in salute.

The marchers returned to the city at twilight, carrying torches and singing a funeral march to the martyrs of February that had been especially composed for the occasion. Its haunting melody and stirring lyrics became enshrined in the hearts of all revolutionaries and would be sung at numerous rallies and demonstrations throughout the course of the Revolution.

You fell in the fatal fight
For the liberty of the people, for the honor of the people
You gave up your lives and everything dear to you,
You suffered in horrible prisons,
You went to exile in chains

Without a word you carried your chains
Because you could not ignore your suffering brothers,
Because you believed that justice is stronger than the sword
The time will come when your surrendered life will count.
That time is near, when tyranny falls, the people will rise, great
　　and free

Farewell, brothers, you chose a noble path,
You are followed by the new and fresh army ready to die and
　　suffer
Farewell, brothers, you chose a noble path,
At your grave we swear to fight,
To work for freedom and the people's happiness

army garrison would sit side by side in the Petrograd Soviet. Russia now had two political centers of power, the Provisional Government and the Petrograd Soviet, whose rivalry was to be the focus of events in the country in the forthcoming months.

THE REVOLUTION TRIUMPHANT

The final collapse of the tsarist government came on Tuesday, February 28. The last remaining loyal troops surrendered or fled the city and the Fortress of Peter and Paul fell without a fight. The insurgents began arresting ministers, generals, and police officers of the old regime. The Provisional Government began to appoint a new cabinet of ministers. Crowds of people celebrated in the streets by dismantling and burning the Romanovs' coat of arms—the double eagle—from buildings and palaces. The Revolution in Petrograd was accomplished with a remarkably small loss of life—only 1,315 people were killed or wounded—a figure that paled in comparison to the hundreds of thousands of Russians who lost their lives in a single battle of the Great War.

The tsarist regime had collapsed, yet Nicholas II still clung to his crown. Although he was only a few hours away from the capital, the events of the five days in Petrograd had completely passed him by. On February 28, the tsar had attempted to head back to Petrograd by train. All day, he traveled from station to station desperately trying to return to his family, but he found that the railroad stations on his route were held by revolutionary forces. So Nicholas rushed to his army headquarters at Pskov, where he ordered his generals to launch a full-scale attack against the Revolution. But the moment for decisive action had long passed. On March 2, his entire general staff, sensing events in the capital were irreversible, deserted the tsar and supported abdication, leaving Nicholas no choice but to renounce his crown. Nicholas tried first to step down in favor of his son, then his brother, the Grand Duke Michael, and finally signed the abdication proclamation on March 2. Yet these attempts at an orderly transition were a hopeless and futile illusion. By the time Nicholas was ready to surrender his crown, the monarchy had already collapsed. As of March 1, 1917, tsarist Russia no longer existed.

CHAPTER FOUR NOTES

p. 41   "The revolutionaries underestimated..." Tsuygoshi Hasegawa. *The February Revolution: Petrograd 1917* (Seattle: University of Washington Press, 1981), p. 217.

p. 43   "We have our husbands, fathers . . ." Hasegawa, p. 234.

p. 45   "Brothers, Cossacks, help the workers . . . " Tsar Nicholas II, quoted in Liebman, p. 102.

p. 46   "I command you to supress . . ." Chamberlin, p. 77.

p. 51   "You fell in the fatal fight . . ." quoted in John Reed. *Ten Days That Shook the World* (New York: Vintage, 1960), p. 178.

DUAL POWER

On March 2, 1917, Paul Miliukov, the head of the liberal Kadet party, appeared before the Petrograd Soviet to read out a list of the complete cabinet appointments to the new Provisional Government. Immediately after he began, a soldier delegate from the audience interrupted his remarks by shouting out: "Who chose you?" It took a brief moment for Miliukov to regain his composure, and when he responded, he made no reference to the Duma or any other elected body. "We were chosen by the Russian revolution," he insisted. "A small group of men was at hand whose past was sufficiently known to the people and against whom there could be no hint of objection." The soldier's frank question, however, pointed to a fundamental dilemma of the February Revolution: namely, that the monarchy had been overturned but the issue of who ruled still hung in the balance.

The political situation in the aftermath of February was completely unprecedented. The country was governed by two separate political institutions, the Provisional Government and the Petrograd Soviet. Although both claimed to speak for the entire nation, each represented a particular social group in society, each had its own aims and beliefs. The Provisional Government was the representative of the upper classes and liberal reformers; the Soviet represented the workers and soldiers. The Provisional Government had been carried to power by the insurgent masses, yet it still considered itself to be the legitimate successor to the deposed tsarist government. The workers and soldiers had effectively overthrown the old regime, yet neither they nor their leaders were prepared to proclaim themselves ready to govern.

What the precise power relationship between these two institutions would be was unclear, as was the course and goals that would direct the future of the Revolution. Would the new Provisional Government reflect the mood and aspirations of Russia's workers and soldiers to seek a social as well as a political transformation, to be revolutionary in fact as well as in name? Or would it carry on the basic tasks of its tsarist predecessor only with greater democracy and efficiency as the liberal leaders of the Provisional Government desired? The competition between the two sides became known as "dual power"; from March until October of 1917, the rivalry inherent in dual power would dominate Russian politics.

THE CHARACTER OF DUAL POWER

The Provisional Government was headed by Prince Georgy Lvov, a former Duma member, but its real leader and intellectual figurehead was Paul Miliukov, who served as minister of foreign affairs. The cabinet was composed primarily of liberals who had distinguished themselves in the Duma. The only minister with even the mildest of progressive tendencies was the young minister of justice, Alexander Kerensky, a 36-year-old lawyer who resigned his place in the Petrograd Soviet to serve in the government.

The Provisional Government's leaders, who had not been elected to power, nevertheless promised to establish a democratic government that offered civil liberties, protection of private property, and an elected legislature. However, this support for liberal democracy was tempered by their fundamental commitment to continue the tsarist policies on the war; they were willing, if necessary, to sacrifice their democratic values in the name of that cause. "The revolution was made for the sole purpose of clearing all obstacles in the path of Russia's victory," wrote Miliukov. The Provisional Government's leaders believed that a democratic administration staffed by able men would mark a tremendous improvement in state efficiency, thereby enabling the nation to fight the war with a much greater chance of success. Of course, the government would face challenging problems in managing the war effort, but the liberal ministers were confident that the greater

The new Provisional Government, including Miliukov (front row right) and Kerensky (top row, second from the right)   (Library of Congress)

popular support given to a democratic regime would make their task considerably easier.

The Petrograd Soviet represented the Russian masses. Its formation provided a springboard for the genuine extension of democracy throughout the rest of the country. Soviets sprang up in every city, town and village; they were quasiparliamentary bodies, intensely engaged in educating the masses in the virtues and practices of democracy and political pluralism. Provisions for regular elections and the periodic recall of all Soviet deputies by their electorate transformed Russia overnight into a nation of enthusiastic voters. At a time when the revolutionary parties, none of whom expected the February Revolution in the first place, were ill prepared to lead the masses, the Petrograd Soviet became the focus of the popular revolution. With nearly 2,000 delegates drawn from factories and army regiments from all over the city, the Soviet served as a critical forum for public debate and competition among the socialist parties. Each party contested for representation in the Soviet and used the Soviet's meetings to promote its political programs. The Mensheviks and Socialist Revolutionaries won huge majorities among the delegates in the initial elections, with the Bolsheviks gaining only a small minority.

The Petrograd Soviet also exercised considerable control over the day-to-day provision of public services. It was widely recognized that the Soviet held the true power in the early days of the Revolution. "The Provisional Government has no real powers. Its orders are not obeyed unless they happen to fall in with the wishes of the Soviet of Workers' and Soldiers' Deputies," admitted War Minister Alexander Guchov. "It is the latter who control the most important aspects of real power: the army, the railways, the postal and telegraph services. One might put it simply that the Provisional Government only exists in as much as the Soviet accepts and authorizes its existence." The paradox of the February Revolution was that the leaders of the Petrograd Soviet showed no interest in challenging the Provisional Government as the lawful political power in revolutionary Russia.

In part, this arose because the moderate socialist leadership of the Petrograd Soviet, following orthodox Marxist theory, believed it was premature to contemplate socialism in such a backward country as Russia. A bourgeois revolution, which the overthrow of the tsar represented, had to be followed by an indefinite period of political rule dominated by the upper classes who would establish a democratic

A meeting of the Petrograd Soviet of Workers' and Soldiers' Deputies (Library of Congress)

regime and promote economic progress. Given that a socialist revolution could not possibly be on the agenda until Russia had become a more economically advanced nation, the demands of the popular revolution could not be so radical as to pose a serious challenge to the bourgeoisie. The liberals should exercise the prominent role in the government, and Soviet power should be used to ensure that the interests of the masses were not ignored. In addition, the Menshevik and SR leaders of the Soviet were also fervent supporters of the war and believed collaboration with the elites was essential to guarantee Russia's survival in the conflict.

In the weeks following the February Revolution, the Provisional Government and the Petrograd Soviet negotiated the broad framework of the political program that was instituted by the Provisional Government in its first weeks. An end to religious or ethnic discrimination, free and open political parties, full amnesty for political prisoners, the abolition of the death penalty, the enactment of civil liberties—all of these were passed in the first rush of legislation. A popular militia was organized to replace the tsarist police and the troops that took part in the revolutionary uprising were given a guarantee that they would not be removed from Petrograd. It was agreed that a national Constituent Assembly would be chosen by universal suffrage later in the year.

It was an admirable beginning yet the joint program was especially notable for what it left unsaid. None of the vital issues that had provoked the revolution in the first place—the war, land reform, or better conditions for workers—were touched upon at all. The liberals and moderate socialists were unable to reach an agreement on these contentious issues, so they decided to postpone all considerations until after the war had been pursued to a victorious conclusion and the Constituent Assembly had been convened. This unwillingness to address the basic political, social, and economic problems of the Russian people was a recipe for disaster. It guaranteed the virtual paralysis of governmental authority and ensured that over time the Provisional Government would forfeit the genuine popularity that it initially enjoyed.

REVOLUTION AND THE WORKING CLASS

In the first dawn of the Revolution, concerns of state appeared far less important than how the daily lives of Russians had been transformed by the events of February. For the Russian masses, the Revolution was a rebirth that marked the banishment of the oppressive and exploitative world of the tsars forever. It engendered a tremendous sense of self-confidence in ordinary Russians. People expanded their political horizons, learned new skills, tested their own limits. For the first time, they read a newspaper or political pamphlet, discussed their own political views with friends, spoke at a mass meeting at their factory or town hall.

In the early days of the Revolution, it was Russia's working class that perhaps best exemplified this transformation. The toppling of the autocracy filled the workers with euphoria. They returned to their work places with the determination to sweep away the tsarist regime in the factory just as it had been swept away in the society as a whole. Tyrannical foremen and police informers were thrown into wheelbarrows and unceremoniously carted out of the factory. "Carting out was a symbolic affirmation," wrote historian S. A. Smith, "by workers of their dignity as human beings and a ritual humiliation of those who had deprived them of this dignity in their day to day working lives."

In place of the old authoritarian structures of power, workers created a new democratic order. Factory committees were established in every work place to provide a collective voice for all workers. These committees supervised hiring and firing decisions, negotiated wages and working conditions, and handled grievances. Each worker regardless of age, skill, or gender was eligible to vote in elections for the committees. Delegates could be recalled by their fellow workers at any time by vote at a general meeting and were required to report back to the workers about their efforts on a regular basis.

Factory committees worked to improve every aspect of workers' lives. Calls for better working conditions or an eight-hour day were seen not merely as a way of diminishing exploitation but as a way to create an environment in which workers would have a greater opportunity to express their full creativity as human beings. Factory committees sought to raise the educational and cultural level of the workers to enable them to be more fully involved in public affairs. They organized evening literacy classes, political lectures, theater performances, and poetry readings. "Let the idea that knowledge is everything sink deeper into our consciousness," said one worker. "It is the essence of life and it alone can make sense of life . . . Do not waste a moment fruitlessly. Every hour is dear to us. We are now the masters of our own lives and so we must become masters of all the weapons of knowledge."

Workers were willing to offer conditional support to the Provisional Government so long as it represented the workers' interests, and this cooperative spirit extended to the factory floor as well. March and April marked an unusual period of conciliation between workers and employers. Most businesses were willing to grant concessions that would ensure peaceful industrial relations, and workers themselves were anxious to regain a measure of stability in their daily lives. After negotiations between the Petrograd Soviet and the Petrograd Society of Industrialists, the capital's businesses agreed to recognize the eight-hour day, minimum wage, trade union rights, and an ample workers' compensation fund. This truce proved only temporary: it would disintegrate under the force of a mounting economic crisis and the radicalization of Russian workers. This radicalization was given a voice by the return on the revolutionary scene of the exiled leader of the Bolshevik party, Vladimir Lenin.

LENIN AT THE FINLAND STATION

The outbreak of the February Revolution had found Vladimir Lenin living in exile in Zurich. He negotiated the approval of the German government to return to Russia aboard a "sealed train," with all communications to the outside world strictly forbidden, that traveled through war-torn Germany and then Finland. On April 3, 1917, Lenin arrived at the Finland Station in Petrograd. The Bolsheviks had made elaborate preparations to transform his arrival into a vivid display of the party's strength and popularity. A brass band played the revolutionary anthem "Marseillaise" and the platform was packed with enthusiastic soldiers and workers waving a sea of red flags and banners. "I am happy to greet you persons of the victorious Russian revolution," he told the crowd, "and salute you as the vanguard of the world wide proletarian army. Any day now the whole of European capitalism may crash. The Russian revolution accomplished by you has paved the way and opened a new epoch. Long live the world wide socialist revolution."

The scene in the square outside the station was pandemonium. Tens of thousands of workers and soldiers filled the square and the adjacent

Vladimir Lenin, leader of the Bolshevik party   (National Archives)

streets. Automobile horns blared, flashlights flickered, and searchlights illuminated the scene. Because it was too crowded to move forward, Lenin jumped atop an armored car and delivered another rousing speech to the cheering crowd. As the car moved off toward Bolshevik headquarters, Lenin was compelled by the ever growing crowds to make a speech at every major crossing. A journey that normally took minutes stretched into hours. He told a delegation of sailors from the Kronstadt base:

> I don't know yet whether you agree with the Provisional Government. But I know very well that when they give you sweet speeches and make many promises they are deceiving you and the whole Russian people. The people need peace. The people need bread and land. And they give you war, hunger, no food, and the land remains with the landowners. Sailors, comrades, you must fight for the revolution, fight to the end.

Lenin's words that evening completely stunned his Bolshevik colleagues and other onlookers. Since the February days, the party had been aligned with the moderate majority in the Petrograd Soviet and had adopted a cautious, uncritical attitude toward the Provisional Government. No one had dared speak of the Provisional Government with such unsparing criticism as Lenin. No one had envisioned the February Revolution in such an explicit international context, as a spark in a much vaster revolutionary upheaval that would soon engulf all of Europe.

Lenin's views were encapsulated in his so-called April Theses. His starting point was that the Provisional Government did not represent the interests of the Russian masses. It was a tool of the privileged classes and no support should be given to its policies. The welfare of Russia's workers, peasants, and soldiers could only be satisfied by a qualitatively different government and a radically new socialist society. The bourgeois revolution of February had reached the end of its course; the onset of revolution in the more advanced nations of Europe, such as Germany, which Lenin believed was imminent, would enable Russia to "skip stages" in the revolutionary process. Henceforth, all power should be transferred immediately over to the Soviets, which would pave the way for a socialist government. So long as the Petrograd Soviet was dominated by the Mensheviks and Socialist Revolutionaries who resolutely refused to assume power, the Bolsheviks' task would be to expose the fraudulence of the Provisional Government and the errors of the moderate socialists.

The Bolshevik Central Committee initially rejected his theses by an overwhelming majority yet in the following weeks, Lenin used all his formidable gifts of persuasion, intelligence, and energy to win over his fellow Bolsheviks. By April 14, his call for a transfer of power to the Soviets was carried by a 20–6 margin. From this time forward the Bolsheviks were the only party in Russia that was completely committed to an extreme left program: if and when the mood of the masses moved leftward, the Bolsheviks would be in place to reap the benefits.

APRIL DAYS

By mid-April, there were growing signs of mass discontent with the Provisional Government and ominous cracks in the revolutionary coalition began to develop. The first indications of tension arose as a result of the deteriorating economic situation. The war had generated massive shortages of housing, food, fuel, and clothing throughout the country. Unfortunately, the February Revolution did not solve these difficulties; on the contrary, the chaotic conditions substantially increased in the first two months after the revolution. Scarcity of essential items significantly worsened by April: food shortages forced a further reduction in bread rations for urban residents, and the lack of raw materials led some factory owners to cut back production and lay off workers.

With poverty and misery again on the rise, there was a marked increase in polarization among social groups. Workers denounced the privileged elites who continued to live in splendid luxury, and openly questioned whether the hopes of the revolution were not being betrayed. Their calls for greater government regulation of the out-of-control economy were vehemently resisted by the Provisional Government and their allies, who began to vent their own criticism about the state of Russian politics. Industrialists chastised workers for their excessive demands and argued that the eight-hour day and trade union freedoms should be repealed. In this atmosphere of mutual blame and suspicion, the truce between workers and employers unraveled.

The issue that truly tested the fragility of dual power, and the legitimacy of the Provisional Government itself, was the bitter conflict

PAUL MILIUKOV

Paul Miliukov was the founder and leader of Russia's liberal party, the Constitutional Democratic party (Kadets). He was born in Moscow in 1859 and became a well-known historian at the University of Moscow. Miliukov was fired for his political activity and was forced to emigrate to America, where he remained for nearly 10 years. While at the University of Chicago, he continued to write against the tsarist regime and warned that the government had "shown itself to be incompatible with the gratification of the most elementary needs."

Upon learning of the events of Bloody Sunday in 1905, Miliukov returned to Russia in April and plunged into revolutionary politics. In the aftermath of the Revolution, he helped form the Kadet party but then he favored change through peaceful and legal methods. Miliukov led the Kadet delegation within the Duma and became a harsh critic of the tsarist regime. He sought to pressure the tsar to enact reforms that would stave off the revolution that he feared was imminent. When World War I began, Miliukov abandoned his previous pacifism and became one of the most ardent supporters of the war.

Miliukov was the dominant political figure in the months after the February Revolution and continually opposed all attempts to deepen the effect of the Revolution by way of social reforms. The Kadets moved sharply to the right in the incredibly polarized atmosphere of the summer of 1917 and would eventually throw their support to efforts at establishing a military dictatorship. After the Bolsheviks' victory in October, Miliukov gave his support to the counterrevolutionary armies and tried in vain to recruit a military force that was capable of deposing the Bolshevik regime. He collaborated with the German forces occupying the Ukraine and traveled extensively throughout Europe to urge greater military intervention by the Allies against the Soviet government. Miliukov eventually settled in Paris, where he continued his writings against the Communist government. He died in 1943.

between the upper and lower classes on the war. The liberal leaders of the government seriously miscalculated the mood of the war weary nation. Since February nothing had happened to revive the taste for military adventure among the Russian masses, who had had enough of the bloody slaughter. Support for the war among the upper and middle classes, on the other hand, was fervent and widespread. The minister of foreign affairs, Miliukov, who dominated the government's diplomacy, remained firmly committed to a continuation of the tsarist war policy. This meant not only staying loyal to the Allies and fighting by their side but also publicly endorsing the secret agreements that provided Russia with war booty in case of an Allied victory.

The Petrograd Soviet leadership opposed the government's embrace of tsarist war aims and supported a continuation of the war only so long as Russian territory was under attack. The Soviet called upon the Provisional Government to renounce its policy, but on March 23, Miliukov publicly affirmed that the government would "irresistibly adhere to their agreement with the Allies." After furious protests from the Soviet, the liberal leaders of the government were forced to retract their original views and publish a statement of war aims that were more in keeping with the Soviet position. This resolution was forwarded to

The April Days (Library of Congress)

the Allies as a statement of official policy, yet Miliukov saw fit to take matters in his own hands. He tried to nullify the implications of the resolution by including a covering note that said there would be no slackening of the war effort and that Russia would respect all its secret obligations.

The publication of the Miliukov note in mid-April unleashed a storm of indignation. Soldiers and workers felt terribly betrayed by the government's double dealings. On April 20 and 21, Petrograd was packed with massive protests and demonstrations. Garrison regiments, workers, and members of the Bolshevik party marched through the streets of the capital with signs reading "Down with the Provisional Government!" ... "Down with Miliukov!" ... "All Power to the Soviets." Army units surrounded the government headquarters and were prepared to arrest the entire cabinet but were dissuaded by delegates from the Soviet.

In the face of such outrage, the Provisional Government was forced to retreat. The note was officially repudiated and Miliukov was made to resign his cabinet post. The April Days demonstrated the continued centrality of the Russian masses in the course of the Revolution; their voices would dominate the next stage of the Revolution as well.

CHAPTER FIVE NOTES

p. 55   "Who chose you . . ." Chamberlin, p. 92.

p. 56   "The revolution was made for . . ." Paul Miliukov, quoted in Liebman, p. 112.

p. 58   "The Provisional Government has . . ." Alexander Guchov, Liebman, p. 114.

p. 60   "Carting out was a symbolic . . ." Smith, p. 57.

p. 60   "Let the idea that knowledge . . ." Smith, p. 95.

p. 61   "I am happy to greet . . ." Vladimir Lenin, quoted in Liebman, p. 108–109.

THE REVOLUTION TURNS TO THE LEFT

The April Days irrevocably altered the political map of revolutionary Russia. Miliukov's resignation sparked a major reorganization of the government: the new cabinet appointed in April now included six socialist ministers, including Irakly Tsereteli as minister of posts and telegraphs and Viktor Chernov as minister of agriculture. Alexander Kerensky was appointed minister of war, and the key foreign affairs post was given to Mikhail Tereshchenko, a well-known industrialist. Although both liberals and moderate socialists warmly greeted the formation of a government that included "all the vital forces of the revolution," it was not immediately evident that this new coalition could solve the fundamental contradictions of dual power.

Both the liberal leaders of the Provisional Government and the moderate socialists of the Petrograd Soviet agreed that the greater legitimacy of the new coalition should be used to convince workers to moderate their claims and persuade the entire population of the need for a renewed military effort. The new coalition believed that if the war was to be fought with any success, then the fighting capacity of the Russian army had to be restored as quickly as possible and the entire

ALEXANDER KERENSKY

Alexander Kerensky was the dominant political figure and last prime minister of the Provisional Government. He was born in Simbirsk in April 1881. His father was a provincial tsarist bureaucrat and the head of the primary school that Lenin attended as a boy. Kerensky went on to receive a law degree and, like many of his generation, became radicalized as a result of his student experiences and by the tragic events of 1905. He joined a secretive SR organization dedicated to the violent overthrow of the tsarist regime and was imprisoned for his activities.

Upon his release, Kerensky forswore these sorts of underground activities and accepted the need to concentrate on peaceful, legal methods of opposition. A flamboyant orator and courtroom tactician, he specialized in defending clients whose cases were likely to cause embarrassment to the regime. His greatest triumph came when he exposed the tsarist government's guilt and callousness in the Lena gold mine massacre, where hundreds of workers were murdered.

Kerensky was elected to the Duma in 1912 as a member of the Trudovik (Labor) party and became the spokesperson for the radical deputies. He attacked the autocracy vociferously throughout the war years for its inability to fight the war successfully but never adopted an antiwar stance of his own.

His former notoriety ensured that Kerensky would be well received by the workers and soldiers who led the February Revolution. He served as minister of justice and minister of war before serving as prime minister for the remainder of the Provisional Government's tenure. His major failing was his unwillingness to break with the unpopular government position on the war, which was beyond the limited capacity of the country. Russia nearly ground to a halt under the pressures of the war, yet Kerensky persisited in an outmoded patriotism that became his downfall. After the Bolshevik uprising, Kerensky emigrated abroad, where he served as the editor of numerous anti-Soviet emigré newspapers. He narrowly escaped from France after the invasion by Nazi Germany in World War II and lived in the United States until his death in 1970.

population must be prepared to make whatever sacrifices were necessary to contribute to victory.

Nevertheless, any coalition government in revolutionary Russia was trapped in a fundamental contradiction. The overriding priority of the liberals was to restore governmental order, renew the war effort, and delay all social change until after the war was won. The moderate socialist leaders of the Soviet, on the other hand, were ready to support the coalition's policy on the war, yet at the same time they had to assure their natural constituencies in the factories, garrisons, and countryside that they were still committed to working toward peace and social reforms. It is very difficult to imagine how two such diverse groups could ever manage to reach a stable consensus, never mind doing so in the face of the deepening social and economic crisis that faced the first coalition government. The severe difficulties that each successive coalition government was to face in the coming months were ultimately the product of these inherent antagonisms of dual power rather than the result of individual failures or a lack of political judgment.

However, in the first weeks of the new coalition government, these difficulties were not yet obvious and both coalition partners were quite hopeful about the government's prospects for success. The first major policy initiative of the coalition was to begin plans for the resumption of active operations in the war. A new offensive had been in the making long before the coalition government was formed, but it received added impetus after the Allies' spring offensive in the West ground to a halt. Coalition leaders counted on a series of quick victories that would bolster the popularity of the government. Yet what everyone overlooked was the dramatic change in the lives of the Russian soldiers that had taken place since the February Revolution, a transformation that made any new military offensive exceedingly problematic.

THE REVOLUTION AND THE ARMY

The relationship between officers and soldiers under the old regime had mirrored the social divisions of the larger society. The peasant soldiers were treated with insolent contempt by their officers, who were drawn primarily from the privileged elites. Officers openly addressed their men as they would a child or pet and used abusive language to their face. Soldiers in turn were required to address their superior officers as "Your excellency" or "Your radiance," and had to answer back with prescribed phrases like "Exactly so, your Honor" or "Happy to serve you, your Honor." The slightest deviation from this ritual would result in severe punishment. Soldiers were flogged across the back with birch rods for these and other trivial offenses.

The troops were subject to a host of petty restrictions and humiliations when they were off duty. They were forbidden to travel in first- or second-class railroad cars. They were banned from restaurants and theaters. They were unable to smoke cigarettes in public spaces. Entrances to public parks had large signs reading: "DOGS AND SOLDIERS FORBIDDEN TO ENTER." Russian soldiers deeply resented these rules and perceived the hierarchy of military authority as repressive and fundamentally illegitimate.

The February Revolution put an end to these humiliating practices and transformed the daily existence of the Russian troops in much the same way as working-class life had been overturned. Reminiscent of the workers' carting out of foremen, soldiers tore off the badges of rank from their most abusive officers. Sailors renamed their ships with names befitting the new revolutionary society: the *Emperor Paul the First* became *The Republic, the Emperor Alexander II* the *Dawn of Liberty*, and the *Nicholas II* was renamed simply *Comrade*.

The Petrograd Soviet moved immediately to safeguard formally these new rights in legislation. The famous Order #1 of the Soviet freed soldiers from tsarist military discipline and gave them the same political and civil rights that other citizens enjoyed outside military service. Standing at attention and compulsory saluting outside of duty were abolished, as were corporal punishment and polite forms of address. The order asserted the Soviet's authority over all policy questions involving the army; no government order was valid unless it was approved by the Soviet as well. It also provided for the democratization of the military through the creation of elected soldiers' committees in every army unit to regulate the behavior of officers and ensure that the soldiers' basic dignity would be respected. This principle of democratic control of the army was vehemently resisted by the officer corps, which believed in their absolute right to command without any political interference. Moreover, they worried that the establishment of two

Soldiers marching through the streets of revolutionary Petrograd (National Archives)

separate authorities within the military would fatally weaken discipline and make a victory in the war more difficult to obtain.

This stubbornness merely confirmed the vast gulf that lay between the average Russian soldier and his officers. The soldiers believed that the February Revolution was an implicit promise that the war would soon come to an end, and they waited impatiently for the Provisional Government to achieve this goal. The sooner the war was over, the sooner these peasant draftees could redeem the promise of the Revolution for an equitable redistribution of the land. A letter from one soldier eloquently summarized their deepest wishes:

> Peace. We dig our graves and call them trenches. What use is freedom to a man in his grave. We will stop this bloody slaughter. This is not our war. We will have an honest, democratic peace, then we can go back to our farms and our factories and put an end to all wars.

However, the coalition's plans for a new military campaign made a mockery of this soldier's aspirations. The Russian offensive began on June 18. Two separate armies launched an attack near the Pripet Marshes against a combined German-Austrian force that had been considerably thinned as a result of transfers to the Western Front. The Russians greatly outnumbered their foes and made spectacular advances in the early moments of the campaign, but once again, the basic incompetence of their generals doomed the effort to failure. After Russia's initial successes, the Germans regrouped and established a strong defensive position. Even so, the Russian leadership continued its fruitless strategy of mounting large frontal attacks against fixed positions. Seventeen futile attempts were made against the German lines at a horrifying cost in lives; more than a quarter of a million soldiers were killed and nearly a million captured.

The death and maiming of a generation of Russia's young men left a terrible scar on the country. Albert Rhys Williams, an American correspondent who lived in Russia during the Revolution, visited a small village in the Ukraine a short time after the offensive began. He was asked to address a crowd of 300 villagers—mostly women, old men and boys, and scores of crippled soldiers. He began by asking the crowd:

"How many of you have ever heard of Washington?" One lad raised his hand. "How many have heard of Lincoln?" Three hands. "Kerensky?" About 90. "Lenin?" Ninety again. "Tolstoy?" One hundred and fifty hands. They enjoyed this, laughing together at the foreigner and his funny accent. Then a foolish blunder. I asked "who of you has lost someone in the war?" Nearly every hand went up, and a wail swept through that laughing throng, like a winter wind moaning in the trees.

This same scene could have been repeated in thousands of Russian villages, each of which had been stripped of their ablebodied men, only to welcome back their sons and husbands physically and mentally crippled from the war.

The June offensive left the army in complete disarray. Desertions reached incredible proportions, with whole regiments surrendering en masse to the enemy. One soldier at the Soviet angrily countered criticism by the Soviet leaders at this breakdown of discipline. "We are not cowards or traitors. But we refuse to fight until we know what we are fighting for," he said. "We are told that this is a war for democracy. We do not believe it."

THE RADICALIZATION OF THE REVOLUTION

The failure of the June offensive highlighted the growing unpopularity of the coalition government among the Russian masses. The conspicuous failure of the government to find a peaceful end to the war led them to believe that the other pressing concerns of the people were likely to be ignored as well. There was a sharp rise in political protest across all social groups and an inevitable crisis of political power.

Although the war acted as the primary catalyst for the deepening political crisis, a severe economic collapse underpinned the crisis. Once again, the symptoms of economic chaos were seen in catastrophic shortages of food, fuel, and raw materials. Food rations in the cities continued to drop every month through the spring and summer. Lines for eggs, sugar, meat, and other precious items began forming at

In the radicalization leading up to the July Days, a protest was held by women for economic reform and an end to the war. (Library of Congress)

midnight, or even nine in the evening, for distribution the following morning. Shops were notoriously understocked, so women workers, who bore the brunt of household duties, spent long hours searching for stores with available supplies and short lines. Even at official prices, people had barely enough money to purchase food, but buying on the black market, where prices were astronomic, was out of the question for most workers. People competed for an ever diminishing stock of food, the price of which rose ever higher and higher.

As inflated prices cut into real wages and the struggle to obtain the bare necessities of life became ever more desperate, workers grew increasingly militant. Workers' demands initially focused on winning higher wages, but it soon became apparent that such a strategy was less and less effective. Higher wages failed to keep pace with inflation and indeed probably fueled it even more. As workers became more combative, many employers chose to shut down their factories rather than deal with their employees' demands. Some spoke openly about taking advantage of the economic crisis to crush the working class once and for all. "To get out of this situation," a leading Moscow industrialist, P. P. Ryabushinsky, was quoted as saying, "we may have to employ the bony arm of hunger, and of natural misery, to take these false friends of the people—the factory committees and Soviets—by the throat."

In this highly volatile atmosphere, and with the traditional methods of struggle seemingly ineffective, Russian workers looked for other forms of struggle to defend their interests. Because they suspected many employers of intentional sabotage, workers began to demand the right to exercise control over management's decisions. (This practice became known as workers' control.) Workers' control was primarily conceived as a pragmatic and defensive response to their precarious position. At first, workers sought to verify employers' claims that raw materials could not be procured, that production had to be curtailed, that workers had to be laid off. Yet the scope of workers' control gradually broadened as the threat of factory closures and layoffs intensified. Factory committees demanded control over the company's sales and finances. In some cases, workers even took over the active management of factories that had been closed down by their owners.

Demand for workers' control inside the factory gates inevitably led to demands for greater governmental control of the national economy as well. Despite their best efforts individual factory committees were barely able to stem the tide of economic chaos. They lacked the necessary funds to buy raw materials or pay the workers' wages, both of which were essential if production were to continue. Worker self-management on its own was also inadequate so long as other employers could refuse to conduct business with workers' enterprises, or ignore their orders, or continue to lay off their own workers.

Yet these calls for more energetic and effective state intervention in the economy came at a time when the coalition government appeared completely ineffectual and its leaders completely unwilling to tolerate the growing radicalism of the workers. Liberals in the government, reflecting their close ties to bankers and industrialists, called on workers to reduce their demands and return to work in the name of "national defense." The moderate socialists likewise rejected demands for greater workers' control as a recipe for economic disaster.

The issue of support for the coalition government soon came to the fore. Workers naturally began to question whether the moderate socialist leaders of the coalition were still willing to take up their cause. "I've had enough of your talking," one worker bluntly informed the Soviet leadership. "You never answer our questions—what are we to do if a boss threatens us he'll close down. You're always ready with proclamations and words, but no one will ever tell us what to do in a real case." Workers and soldiers were deeply disenchanted with the status quo, yet the Soviet leaders continued to exaggerate the potential for painless compromise.

There was one political party prepared to reap the benefits of the workers' and soldiers' dissatisfaction—the Bolsheviks. Since Lenin's return in April, the Bolsheviks had adamantly refused all collaboration with the Provisional Government, and as a consequence, they had been untainted by any of its failures on the economy or the war. The party's platform, concisely summarized in their familiar slogan—peace, land, and bread—offered a distinct alternative. For soldiers at the front, the Bolshevik's denunciation of the war and their embrace of an immediate unconditional peace, held out the promise of a safe return to their homes. For the workers, the Bolshevik's support of workers' control and greater state regulation of the economy, held out the promise of an answer to the economic crisis and a guarantee of decent working conditions and wages. Their slogan "All Power to the Soviets" called for the elimination of the Provisional Government and the promotion of the Soviets to complete political power.

THE JULY DAYS

Amid such a climate of ferment and agitation, it was widely anticipated that a clash between the government and the Bolshevik-inspired workers and soldiers was inevitable. In late June, the resignation of five liberal ministers effectively brought down the first coalition government. It seemed to many workers and soldiers that this now opened the door for the formation of an all-socialist government, but the moderate Soviet leaders looked to negotiate a solution to the crisis that would enable the liberals to return to the cabinet. The radical sections of the workers and soldiers accordingly decided that the time was ripe to turn up the pressure on the coalition government.

On July 3, soldiers from the First Machine Gun Regiment crisscrossed the city, canvassing garrisons and factories for support for an uprising against the regime. They commandeered motorcars and armored vehicles and roamed throughout the city in full dress uniform and battle gear. Brief clashes occurred between the demonstrators and the police and government loyalists; the crowds fled in panic several times after sporadic firing broke out. By early evening, thousands of soldiers and workers were demonstrating outside the Soviet and the Provisional Government headquarters. The government was virtually helpless: there had not been sufficient time to alert loyalist troops at the front to return to the capital and even those regiments that had remained neutral in their barracks during the day's protests were nonetheless reluctant to come to the government's defense.

The Petrograd Soviet leadership supporting the government vehemently condemned the demonstrations as an intimidation of the Soviet's authority. The moderate socialists were convinced that neither the rural provinces nor the army at the front would support a transfer of power to the Soviets. They also believed that any break with the upper classes would fatally weaken the war effort and enhance the

Insurgents run for their lives under fire during the July Days. (National Archives)

likelihood of a counterrevolution. However, crowds gathered outside the Soviet headquarters throughout the night, ignoring the appeals of the Soviet leaders to return to their garrisons and homes. The spirit of the insurgents was perhaps best characterized by the soldier who shook his fist at the SR Minister Chernov and yelled: "Take power you son of a bitch when they give it to you!"

The July Days reached their peak on the afternoon of July 4. Nearly 400,000 soldiers and workers participated in demonstrations in the capital. The mood among the insurgents was highly volatile: everyone seemed on edge, uncertain of what would happen next, impatient for a definitive resolution to the crisis. Was this the decisive uprising that would install a Soviet regime or would the government recover in time?

Many of the protestors looked to the Bolsheviks for leadership in the struggle, yet the party was in an untenable and unenviable position. It had to decide whether to seize power by force, riding the wave of insurgency of the workers and soldiers, or else make a concerted effort to end the demonstrations. At the moment, there appeared to be several reasons why restraint might be the wisest option. The Bolsheviks did not yet enjoy any substantial support among the peasants, nor could they expect the unanimous support of the troops at the front. A premature insurrection would leave Petrograd terribly isolated from the rest of the country and it was unlikely that a revolutionary government limited to just the capital could hold out for long. Nor could they seize power independently of and against the opposition of the Petrograd Soviet so long as its leadership enjoyed the majority support of the soldiers. Many of the garrison troops who participated in the protests had already returned to their barracks and a substantial number of garrisons had refused to choose sides at all.

There were two factors that ultimately tipped the balance in favor of a hasty retreat. The Bolsheviks learned that because of the unwillingness of some garrisons to come to the aid of the government, the Petrograd Soviet had ordered troops from the front to the capital. These units were already underway by the late afternoon and the party leadership recognized that any uprising would be suicidal under such circumstances.

Word also leaked to the party that high-level officials within the government were ready to accuse Lenin of being a German agent and of having organized the insurrection at the Germans' behest. The government's counterespionage bureau had fabricated documents and testimony implicating Lenin, and they leaked this material to conservative newspapers. They hoped that by branding Lenin a traitor, they would discredit his and the Bolsheviks' reputation among the garrison soldiers and thus enlist them in the support of the regime. By evening there were growing signs that the campaign of innuendo, which would be splashed across the front pages of Petrograd's newspapers the following morning, had already persuaded several garrisons to withdraw their neutrality and go over to the government's side.

By the morning of July 5, Bolshevik newspapers were calling for an immediate halt to further strikes and demonstrations but by then most soldiers had already returned to their garrisons. The July Days, which to quote Lenin were "considerably more than a demonstration and less than a revolution," turned out to be an unqualified disaster for the Bolshevik party. The government and its allies would use the aborted uprising as an opportunity to launch a full-scale repression against the Bolsheviks and the left. It seemed to many observers that the left's role in the Revolution had reached a dead end.

CHAPTER SIX NOTES

p. 74   "How many of you have ever . . ." Quoted in Albert Rhys Williams, *Through the Revolution* (New York: Monthly Review Press, 1967), pp. 65–66.

p. 76   "To get out of this situation . . . " P. P. Ryabushinsky, quoted in Chamberlin, pp. 267–268.

p. 77   "I've had enough . . . " Smith, p. 166.

p. 79   "Take power you . . ." Chamberlin, p. 171.

p. 80   "considerably more than a . . ." Lenin, quoted in Chamberlin, p. 178.

CHAPTER 7

THE SPECTER
OF REACTION

The aftermath of the July Days ushered in a profound shift to the right in the political climate of the Revolution. In sharp contrast to their euphoria in June and July, workers and soldiers appeared completely demoralized and disenchanted about the prospects of further revolutionary change. The resolve and confidence of the elites and government officials, on the other hand, had never been higher. The abrupt demise of the July uprising put them in a much stronger position than ever before, and they were intent on pressing this advantage against their adversaries on the left to the fullest. "The difference in mood between July 4th and 5th is so enormous," wrote one reporter, "it is misleading to refer to it as a change, it is as if we had suddenly been transported from one city to another and found oneself amidst different people and different moods."

THE JULY REACTION

Upper-class circles had exerted considerable pressure on the Provisional Government to suppress the left as far back as April. The opening shot in the new attack was the smear campaign the government mounted against Lenin and the Bolsheviks as German agents, a charge that had been raised against the Bolshevik leader ever since he returned to revolutionary Russia through the assistance of Germany.

When the official government archives were opened after World War II, it was revealed that Germany had indeed diverted huge sums of money to the Russian revolutionaries with the obvious intent of disrupting Russian politics. Some of these funds undoubtedly ended up in the Bolshevik coffers, but there was no evidence that the leaders of

LEON TROTSKY

Leon Trotsky, a prolific writer, gifted orator, and energetic organizer, was, alongside Lenin, the outstanding leader of the Bolshevik Revolution. He was born Lev Bronstein in 1870 in a small rural town in the Ukraine, the son of a prosperous Jewish farmer. Like Lenin, the young Trotsky grew up in comfortable conditions and was first drawn to socialism after being caught up in the ferment of revolutionary protest at university. He threw himself into radical politics but was sent into exile in Siberia, from which he escaped in order to join the Russian social democrats abroad.

The 22-year-old revolutionary met Lenin in London in 1902 and immediately became one of the featured writers for the Russian Social Democratic newspaper. However, within a year, he and Lenin had a harsh falling out over Lenin's general conception of the revolutionary party, which Trotsky believed contained the seeds of dictatorship. The two men were bitter political rivals for years and assailed each other's political philosophy and personal character. Trotsky became an isolated political figure, a member of neither the Bolsheviks nor the Mensheviks, though his greatest triumph occurred during the 1905 Revolution, when he served as the president of the first Petrograd Soviet.

When the tsar was overthrown, Trotsky was living in New York City, but he made an immediate impression upon arriving in Petrograd in May 1917. He affirmed his support for Lenin's April Theses and formally joined the Bolshevik party, which appointed him to its Central Committee. With Lenin in hiding after the July Days debacle, it was Trotsky who became the dominant figure of the revolutionary left, taking firsthand the party were implicated in the transactions or, more importantly, that their behavior was in any way swayed by "German gold." Nonetheless, the impression given by the scandal was devastating. "Appearances spoke against Lenin," wrote historian Marcel Liebman, "and for the moment appearances were decisive."

control of the preparations for the insurrection and mobilizing support for the Soviet through his marvelous oratory. His role during the Civil War was equally impressive. Trotsky single-handedly molded the ragtag force of Red Guards into the five-million-strong Red Army that saved the Soviet regime. His exploits aboard the military train that took him from front to front became legendary. An original and unorthodox military tactician and strategist, Trotsky took personal charge of several key campaigns, including the defense of Petrograd in 1919, where by his inexhaustible energy and moral fervor, he was able to rally the Red forces to a victory that saved the city from capture.

The Civil War represented the pinnacle of Trotsky's revolutionary career: in the remaining two decades of his life, he was destined to become a heroic figure condemned to a life befitting a Greek tragedy. In the 1920s, Trotsky became embroiled in a bitter fight with Joseph Stalin to succeed Lenin as the head of the Soviet government. He urged greater democracy within the Communist party, a revival of Soviet democracy, and the renewal of revolutionary internationalism, but he was outmaneuvered in the power struggle by Stalin, who became the absolute dictator of the Soviet Union.

After 1929, Trotsky was exiled to Norway and France and eventually took refuge in Mexico, where he condemned Stalin's policies of terror as a betrayal of the revolutionary hopes of 1917. As a consequence, Stalin eradicated Trotsky from Soviet histories of the Revolution. He was excised from photographs of the period, and all of his writings were banned. Trotsky wrote numerous books on the Russian Revolution and the contemporary political history of the 1930s; his three-volume history of the Revolution remains a classic to this day. He was assassinated in 1940 by a member of Stalin's secret police.

The Provisional Government did not stop short at slander. The Bolshevik newspaper offices were ransacked and its printing presses dismantled. Local activists were beaten up and arrested, and the Red Guards (Bolshevik militias) were outlawed. Bolshevik leaders such as Leon Trotsky and Lev Kamenev were imprisoned and a warrant was issued for Lenin's arrest. Lenin feared assassination and fled to a small village in Finland, 20 miles northwest of the capital, where he would remain until late September. "The Bolsheviks are compromised, discredited and crushed," one conservative newspaper gloated. "More than that, they have been expelled from Russian life, their teaching has turned out to be an irreversible failure and has scandalized itself and its believers before the world and for all time."

The crackdown against the Bolsheviks was mirrored by the actions of other sectors to stem the tide of the radicals. The Russian military command sharply curtailed the authority of the soldiers' committees, banned all political meetings and Bolshevik propaganda, and decided to dissolve the Petrograd garrisons that had participated in the uprising. Industrialists were markedly more strident in their demands for greater labor discipline. They were unanimous in their calls for a "strong government" that would prohibit strikes and street demonstrations, and would weaken the institutions of the revolutionary democracy.

The collapse of the first coalition during the July Days left the question of political power once again hanging in the balance. The moderate socialists gave full approval to the government's sanctions against the Bolsheviks; Tsereteli, one of the socialist ministers, condemned them as "traitors who stabbed democracy in the back and played into the hands of the counterrevolution." The moderate socialists reluctance to seize power on their own drove them into an even closer alliance with the liberals. Kerensky, who was named the new prime minister, was given a free hand in the aftermath of the crisis to negotiate a new coalition, and he assembled a government that closely resembled its predecessor. The socialists enjoyed a numerical majority in the cabinet but the most powerful posts were monopolized by the Liberals, who this time were prepared to exact a steep price for their further participation in the government. They insisted that land reform and the convocation of the Constituent Assembly should be postponed until after the war was won. They demanded that the socialist ministers pledge their independence from the Petrograd Soviet and abandon all proposals of social reform. The Kadets hoped to eventually eliminate the influence of the Soviet altogether, and this policy was viewed sympathetically by Kerensky, who assured the British ambassador that "the Soviet will die a normal death."

Both the liberals and socialists pledged their support for a "strong government" that would do whatever was necessary to restore order in the country. Little did they know that developments in the Russian countryside would soon make a mockery of this show of authority.

THE REVOLUTION AND THE PEASANTRY

While revolutionary momentum may have come to a standstill in the rest of the country, the summer of 1917 marked the full-scale radicalization of the peasantry. Like Russia's soldiers and workers, the peasants used the Revolution to democratize their daily lives. In the first days of the Revolution, open assemblies of villagers met to discuss the new situation and formulate resolutions on a broad range of issues: the future of the war, food prices, land redistribution. These assemblies eventually evolved into peasant committees elected by all village inhabitants. Under the old regime, peasant politics had been dominated by the male elders of the commune: this undemocratic system reflected patriarchal relations within peasant households in which the authority of the eldest male was unquestioned. The peasant committees were revolutionized by the inclusion of new groups: women, landless laborers, village teachers and doctors, and soldiers returning home on leave.

The Revolution empowered the peasants to assert their own authority and control over all matters affecting their lives. The peasant committees replaced the old repressive institutions of tsarism that had made peasants' lives so miserable. Peasant committees created their own police force, court system, educational system, and organizations of local governance. They regulated rental agreements with landlords, prohibited land sales to absentee landlords, and boycotted tax collections. The committees began to tentatively challenge the rights of the gentry: wood owned by nobles was chopped down without permission or payment, peasant cattle were put out to pasture in landlords' fields, rent payments were held back. Some of the bolder committees began repossessing and redistributing the land of the most exploitative nobles.

Like all social groups, Russia's peasants saw the fall of the tsar as a signal that their long-standing grievances would be redressed and their deepest held aspirations would be realized. The peasants' strongest desire was for the land to belong to those who worked it and no one else. This meant that the illegitimate title of the nobles to the land would be revoked and private landowners would retain no more than the area of land that they could work with their own labor. Absentee landlords would likewise be dispossessed and the authority of the peasant commune reasserted.

However, this kind of radical land reform was not immediately forthcoming. Liberals in the coalition feared any substantive program of land reform would entice peasant soldiers to desert their posts. The SR leaders of the coalition, whose radical program of land reform was extremely popular throughout the countryside, refused to implement their own party policies for fear of alienating their coalition partners and of jeopardizing the war effort. The procrastination of the Provisional Government on every important issue rapidly eroded its credibility among the peasantry. In the spring a peasant delegation met with Kerensky to seek a law that would ban the widespread sale of land to absentee landlords. The prime minister told them he could make no promises except to say that the government would take "all the necessary measures." When one of the peasants pointed out that such a law had already been promised but nothing had been done, Kerensky interrupted furiously. "I said it would be done and that means it will be," said the prime minister. "And there is no need to look at me so suspiciously."

By mid-summer the peasants decided to take matters into their own hands and plunged the entire Russian countryside into the throes of rebellion. Under the direction of the peasant committees, they seized the estates of nobles and landlords. Peasants first gathered in the village square and then proceeded toward an estate carrying pitch forks, axes, and rifles. The squire of the property, if he had not already fled, was placed under arrest and forced to sign over his property. Consistent with traditional practice, the land was divided equally among all villagers. In some cases, the landlord was attacked and the estate buildings burned to the ground in order to ensure that the transfer of the land could never be reversed. One peasant explained what the aim was: "The muzhiki [peasants] are destroying the squires' nests so that the little bird will never be able to return"—the "bird" here referring to landlords of large estates. This virtual state of rebellion was looked upon with considerable apprehension by the government, yet they were powerless to intervene. The army was too unreliable to use to crush the seizures because the soldiers overwhelmingly sympathized with their fellow peasant's desire for land.

A GENERAL ON HORSEBACK

The rebellion in the countryside was merely one aspect of the deepening social and political crisis that threatened Russia by the end of the summer. Despite all its pretensions of enacting "strong measures," the second coalition appeared to be afflicted with the same fatal paralysis of political leadership that had doomed its predecessor. It took no decisive action to repair the disintegrating economy and continued unchanged a discredited war policy that offered no favorable outcome. It was unable to stem the tide of peasant agitation that was laying waste to the great estates of the Russian countryside. Similarly, if the new coalition's primary objective from the outset had been to crush the left, its performance in this regard had been a mixed blessing. The regime had intended to dismantle all those radical garrisons that had been instrumental in the July uprising, yet by early August, not a single one had been dissolved. Although many of its top leaders had been imprisoned or were in hiding, the Bolshevik party had not been outlawed and they steadily regained their old influence among the workers and soldiers.

These developments led many business elites, army officers, conservative politicians, even the majority of liberals, to conclude that the only hope of restoring order at the front and curbing protest in the rear was to establish a dictatorship. Only strong, repressive, measures that eliminated every vestige of power on the part of the revolutionary democracy—the army commissars, factory and peasant committees, and the Soviets—would restore political order. Some hoped Kerensky could be convinced to implement the stern measures while others, primarily monarchist groups and representatives of the officer corps, went further in pledging their outright support for a military coup d'etat against the Provisional Government.

The search for a "general on horseback," a strong leader who could take on the mantle of dictator, settled upon General Lavr Kornilov, who had been appointed commander in chief in July. Kornilov had little political experience and no understanding of the complexity of Russian political life. He saw no difference between the moderate socialists who supported the war and the Bolsheviks who adamantly opposed it. His intelligence was not widely admired either: a fellow general described him as "a man with a lion's heart and the brain of a sheep." Nevertheless, the general was viewed by many as the natural successor to Kerensky. In fact, there was little politically that separated the two men. By mid-August Kerensky was prepared to adopt policies that were virtually indistinguishable from those proposed by Kornilov. The rivalry between the two men was primarily the result of naked ambition. Both were equally committed to an authoritarian government, yet each man saw himself as the only authentic leader of such a regime.

It was not their individual ambitions that drove a wedge between the two leaders but rather a minor farce of comic misunderstandings, provoked by a blundering intermediary named V. N. Lvov, a former deputy in the Duma. In a series of meetings between August 22 and 26, Lvov managed to convince Kerensky that the general was actively plotting a coup d'etat against the government and to convince Kornilov that the prime minister was willing to surrender all power to the general. In the resulting confusion, Kerensky had Lvov arrested and dismissed Kornilov as commander in chief on the morning of August 27. Kornilov was bewildered by Kerensky's sudden turnaround, and he had absolutely no intention of stepping down as the head of the army. Several weeks earlier Kornilov had secretly ordered a number of his regiments to move within striking distance of Petrograd in preparation for a coup. Now he gave these troops the order to move on the capital: Kornilov intended to place the city under martial law, disperse the Soviets and all other democratic organizations, and arrest all political opponents. He confidently predicted an easy victory to his general staff. "No one will defend Kerensky," he said. "This will be a promenade." Yet once again, both Kornilov and his supporters seriously underestimated the mood and critical importance of the Russian masses, whose timely intervention would turn the tide in favor of the Revolution.

THE KORNILOV COUP

Late in the day of August 27, the Petrograd Soviet leadership learned of the impending coup d'etat. With Kornilov's troops already on the move, the Soviet leaders believed they had no choice except to offer their full support to Kerensky; accordingly, they approved of the prime minister appointing a new emergency government. Only the Bolsheviks objected to the socialists' continued support of Kerensky. "The provisional government created the conditions for the counterrevolution," said one Bolshevik leader. "Only the realization of a decisive program—a republic, peace and bread—can instill in the masses confidence in the government." Despite their disagreements, all sides realized that the most pressing task was to prepare for the immediate defense of the capital. The Petrograd Soviet formed an organization called the Committee for the Struggle Against the Counterrevolution to coordinate its military campaign, with the membership shared equally among the Mensheviks, SRs, and Bolsheviks. The inclusion of the Bolsheviks on the committee was a grudging recognition of the party's strong influence among the masses.

The committee's first course of business was to issue orders to all military units that only the instructions of the Soviet were to be respected. Arms and ammunition were distributed to all garrisons. The Red Guards, made up of armed brigades of factory workers, were resurrected and nearly 25,000 new recruits flocked to their ranks within days. Workers were sent to the outskirts of the city to dig trenches and erect barricades. Meanwhile, telegraph workers refused to transmit messages to Kornilov's troops, and railroad workers did all they could to sabotage the progress of his forces. They redirected army trains onto abandoned lines, destroyed tracks, and felled trees across the tracks.

Kornilov's regiments reached within 40 miles of the capital. His troops were stranded, unable to move forward, and unable to communicate with any other units. The soldiers were met by groups of Soviet agitators who berated them for betraying the Revolution. They told Kornilov's troops that their leaders had deceived them, that they were fighting for the wrong cause, that Kornilov wanted to restore the hated ways of the old regime. Kornilov's troops, who had not been informed of why they were attacking Petrograd, had little sympathy for their leader and were unanimous in their support of the authority of the

Soviet. They hoisted red flags atop their army headquarters and arrested their officers. The entire coup collapsed without the firing of a single shot. Kornilov was arrested and the Revolutionary workers and soldiers of Petrograd celebrated their triumph.

The utter collapse of the Kornilov coup demonstrated the changeable nature of the Revolution: in just two months, the political balance of forces had been completely transformed. The Kadet party, which had dominated every Provisional Government since March, was totally discredited by their role in the affair. Although they had not actively instigated any conspiratorial plots within the capital, the party had nonetheless made no secret of its sympathy for Kornilov. On the day of Kornilov's offensive, the Kadet's newspaper, *Rech*, was forced to publish a huge blank space on its front page in place of the leading article that Miliukov had written to welcome Kornilov. Kerensky's reputation was irreparably damaged as well. The right condemned him for betraying their interests, and the left mistrusted him for his ambiguous behavior in the weeks leading up to the coup. The only group to emerge unscathed from the Kornilov affair was the Soviet, whose prestige and authority among the population had never been higher.

The defeat of Kornilov created an unprecedented opportunity for an all-socialist government that would work toward a common revolutionary program to bring an immediate end to the war and greater state control over the disintegrating economy. Popular support for such a regime had never been higher. Two successive coalition governments had failed to enact significant reforms or to stop the war, and most workers and soldiers felt as if the Revolution had reached a standstill. The moderate socialists held the key to the question of political power yet they were still deeply divided on the issue of a socialist government. Although the Kornilov affair convinced them that the Kadets should be banned from participation in the government, they still insisted on the principle that had guided their policies since the first day of the Revolution: that a revolutionary government had to include representatives of the upper classes. "Transfer of power to the revolutionary democracy," said Tsereteli, "without the support of other social groups will be the defeat of democracy; a Soviet takeover of power is ardently awaited by the enemies of the revolution." On September 2, the Executive Committee of the Petrograd Soviet rejected calls for an all-socialist government and agreed to support a new coalition government headed once again by Kerensky.

It was a fateful decision yet one that was not entirely unexpected. The moderate socialists were ultimately constrained by the weight of the choices they had made since the onset of revolution. To now embrace the Bolshevik proposals for an all-socialist government meant repudiating their own policies of the previous six months. It would have signified a willingness on their part to form a new political regime that would be prepared to take full responsibility for maintaining civil order and rebuilding the economy. Such a regime would need to satisfy demands for immediate social reform and peace, knowing full well that this would provoke the determined opposition of industrialists and large landowners. For socialist parties so enamored of social peace and wedded to an ideal of a democratic government made up of all classes, none of these responsibilities was likely to prove attractive. Yet their unwillingness to travel down this path left the moderate socialists fatally isolated from their own constituents and surrendered the initiative for the Revolution to their bitter rivals, the Bolsheviks, who were the only party willing to represent the masses' interests.

CHAPTER SEVEN NOTES

p. 83   "The difference in mood . . ." Quoted in Alexander Rabinowitch. *The Bolsheviks Come to Power: The Revolution of 1917 in Petrograd* (New York: Norton 1978), p. 42.

p. 85   "Appearances spoke against Lenin . . ." Liebman, p. 177.

p. 86   "The Bolsheviks are compromised . . ." Quoted in Rabinowitch, p. 51.

p. 86   "traitors who stabbed . . ." Tsereteli, quoted in Rabinowitch, p. 24.

p. 87   "the Soviet will die . . ." Kerensky, quoted in Liebman, p. 195.

p. 88   "I said it would be done . . ." Kerensky, quoted in Nikolai Sukhanov. *The Russian Revolution 1917* (New York: Harper and Row 1962), p. 328.

p. 90   "a man with a lion's . . ." Rabinowitch, p. 97.

CHAPTER 8

RED OCTOBER

The Bolsheviks' political resurgence since July was nothing short of miraculous. Given up for dead just two months earlier, the party by September had captured the imagination of the Russian masses. By early September, it had won a majority of the deputies in both the Petrograd and Moscow Soviets and made spectacular gains in many regional Soviets as well. While the moderate socialist parties were in a virtual state of paralysis, with a shrinking membership and sparsely attended meetings, the Bolshevik party membership exploded from 60,000 in July to nearly 250,000 by early October. Its newspapers circulated widely and were avidly read by workers and soldiers. Its agitators could be found in every factory and garrison hammering home the Bolsheviks' message.

The party's turnaround testified once again to the enormous attraction of the Bolsheviks' program. The popularity of the Bolsheviks was due precisely to their acute sensitivity to the political attitudes of the Russian working class and soldiers. Their slogan of "peace, land, and bread" was the clearest expression of the aspirations of the Russian masses. As the only party to unequivocally endorse the immediate transfer of governmental power to the Soviets, to pledge an immediate end to the war, and to support the peasant land seizures and radical land reform, the Bolsheviks pledged to renew the Revolutionary hopes that appeared stalled after the successive failures of each coalition government. Most Bolsheviks believed that in the not too distant future the Soviets would be compelled to take steps toward the formation of a Soviet government.

LENIN'S CALL FOR INSURRECTION

Against this background, one can only imagine the extraordinary shock within the Bolshevik party leadership when they received Lenin's letters on September 12 and 14 calling on the party to abandon its peaceful positions in favor of an immediate armed insurrection against the Provisional Government. The Bolshevik leader had consistently endorsed the party's overall strategy in private and public and there had been no hint or warning of such a radical shift in his thinking. However, Lenin was now persuaded that there had been a qualitative shift in the political situation since the Kornilov defeat, and he used these letters to outline his arguments to his party colleagues.

"All the objective conditions exist," wrote Lenin, "for a successful insurrection." The continuing disintegration of the army and the peasant rebellion wreaking havoc in the countryside demonstrated the fundamental weakness of the Provisional Government. The spectacu-

A sign reading "Peace and Brotherhood of the Peoples" hangs over a Bolshevik meeting place. (National Archives)

A HISTORY OF THE RUSSIAN REVOLUTION

lar advance of Bolshevik popularity evidenced by the recent Soviet elections proved the party was not nearly as isolated as it had been in July. Lenin was convinced Europe was on the verge of revolution: he pointed to reports of mutinies in the German navy and food riots in German cities as proof that a revolutionary regime in Russia might provide the spark for revolutions across all of Europe. Lenin urged the party to organize an insurrection at once while their support was at its height and their adversaries at their weakest.

Lenin's bold views encountered the same sort of incredulity and outrage among his colleagues that had greeted his April Theses. Some Bolsheviks, such as Lev Kamenev and Gregory Zinoviev, believed Lenin woefully overestimated the possibility of revolutionary success outside Russia. Others in the party, who regularly interacted with the workers and soldiers and knew of their deep attachment to the revolutionary democratic organizations, cautioned against any move by the Bolsheviks that might be seen as an attack on the legitimacy or authority of the Soviet. The entire leadership worried that if Lenin's views leaked out, the government might use them to justify a new campaign of repression against the left. Accordingly, the Central Committee decided to burn both letters, and in their place, they published several articles Lenin had written weeks earlier when he was still espousing more moderate views.

In late September, Lenin returned secretly to Petrograd and moved to an apartment on the outskirts of the capital. His patience was at the breaking point: for weeks, he had waited anxiously for the party to publish his call for an insurrection but nothing had been forthcoming. Lenin sent a series of stinging rebukes to the Central Committee, charging that their hesitancy was an act of betrayal. He insisted the Bolsheviks had tried every possible method to win the moderate socialists over to a peaceful transition to an all-socialist government, yet they had continually rejected such a course. Lenin threatened to resign from the party leadership and take his case directly to the membership unless the Central Committee agreed to debate his proposals.

On the evening of October 10, the Bolshevik Central Committee bowed to Lenin's pressure and convened a secret meeting to take up the issue of insurrection. No minutes of the meeting exist to convey what must have been an extraordinarily tense atmosphere. It was the first face-to-face confrontation between Lenin and his comrades since his return from Finland. For over 10 hours the party leadership huddled in a dimly lit dining room and debated the question of an armed insurrection. Lenin spent two hours summarizing the case for an immediate uprising, echoing the arguments of his earlier writings. Kamenev and Zinoviev raised their own familiar objections, while others reported on the mood of the workers and soldiers. As the discussion progressed, it became clear that the real debate was not whether the Bolsheviks should overthrow the Provisional Government but how soon and in what fashion.

Early in the morning, the weary Bolshevik leaders voted by a margin of 10–2 to commit the party to an armed insurrection against the government. The Revolution had shifted irrevocably, and once again Lenin's personal contribution was immeasurable. By virtue of his energetic and insistent lobbying, and by his strength of will and intellect, Lenin ultimately succeeded in bringing a majority of the party leaders over to a policy which they had adamantly resisted. "Few modern historical episodes," wrote Alexander Rabinowitch, "better illustrate the sometimes decisive role of an individual in historical events."

ON THE EVE OF INSURRECTION

Although the historic vote of October 10 committed the Bolshevik party to an armed uprising, it by no means guaranteed the success of such a venture. While the masses of soldiers and workers may have been broadly sympathetic to the Bolshevik program, it did not necessarily follow that they would be prepared to take the greater risk of joining or supporting a Bolshevik-led uprising. Nor was there any agreement within the party about when or how the proposed insurrection should take place.

In the second week of October, Kerensky unthinkingly played into the hands of the Bolsheviks. He announced a plan to transfer the bulk of the Petrograd garrison to the front in response to the Germans' capture of two strategically placed islands in the Gulf of Finland, which posed a serious threat to the capital. Kerensky expected the heightened danger would create widespread support for his decision to purge the garrison's most radical elements, yet his announcement unleashed a wave of indignation. The entire Petrograd garrison voted for an immediate transfer of power to the Soviets; even those regiments who had been reluctant to support the Bolsheviks in July were now ready to pledge their complete loyalty to the Bolshevik-dominated Soviet. The Soviet formed a new defense organization, the Military Revolutionary Committee (MRC), which countermanded Kerensky's order and commanded the garrison to assume battle readiness.

By mid-October, the entire country seemed on edge, with wild rumors circulating everywhere about the uprising that the Bolsheviks were supposedly hatching. An endless topic of conversation and speculation on street corners and store lines and at dinner tables was whether the Bolsheviks were "ready to go." On October 18, these widespread suspicions were seemingly confirmed once and for all when Zinoviev and Kamenev, who had been unable to raise their objections to the proposed uprising in the Bolshevik party press, published a joint article in an independent newspaper that revealed the party's secret vote in favor of an uprising.

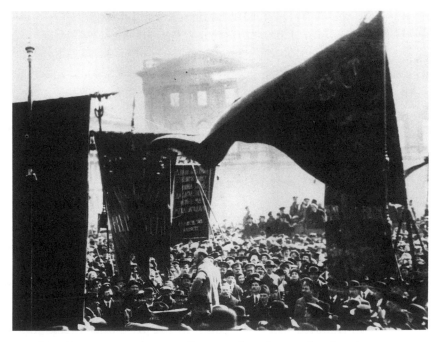

A Bolshevik agitator at a factory rally in October   (National Archives)

Despite such irrefutable evidence about the Bolshevik's plans, the Kerensky government was curiously nonchalant, even rashly overconfident, about its political fortunes. "I could pray that such an uprising would take place," Kerensky cockily bragged. "I have more strength than I need. They will finally be smashed." Yet as of the third week of October, there had been few active measures taken by the government to either weaken the Bolsheviks or strengthen its own defenses in the event of an uprising. There had been no survey of the Petrograd garrison to find out which regiments were still loyal to Kerensky, no attempt to move extra troops into the capital.

Meanwhile, the Bolsheviks were furiously organizing the masses behind the scenes. They secretly organized and trained Red Guard units, and party agitators visited factories and garrisons to promote the call for an all-socialist government. The party's finest orators crisscrossed the city, speaking at factory meetings and numerous mass rallies. On October 22, the House of the People was jammed with soldiers and workers who had come to see the featured speaker, Trotsky, who was legendary for his extraordinary oratory. For over an hour, the Bolshevik leader held his audience spellbound with his vision of the socialist future about to dawn. "The Soviet regime will give everything that is in the country to the poor and to the people in the trenches," he said. "You, bourgeoisie have two coats—hand one over to the soldier who is cold in the trenches. You have warm boots? Sit at home—the worker needs your boots." Trotsky asked the enthusiastic crowd "to support the Soviet that has taken on itself the glorious burden of bringing the victory of the revolution to a conclusion, and of giving peace, land and bread!"

The day before Trotsky's speech, a series of events ensued that proved critical for the momentum hurtling Russia toward another revolution. On October 21, the leaders of the MRC declared that unless they were given authority to countersign all orders given to the Petrograd garrison, they would instruct every regiment in the capital to disobey orders issued by the government. The military commander of the Petrograd district refused their ultimatum, so the MRC dispatched its own commissars to every Petrograd garrison to ensure that no orders would be accepted without the MRC's permission.

By October 23, it was clear that the government's position had seriously deteriorated. Reports began to pour into the Winter Palace about the gigantic rallies held around the city the night before in support of the Soviet and the Bolsheviks. Officers complained that their troops were already refusing orders at the behest of the Soviet commissars. The time for decisive action could no longer be delayed, still Kerensky vacillated. He ordered the arrest of prominent Bolsheviks and the MRC leaders but allowed himself to be talked out of such a move by his cabinet. He called upon the general staff to prepare troops at the front for a rapid move on the capital but was told that soldiers at the front were unwilling to fight against the Soviet under any circumstances. Everyone within the government continued to blindly underestimate the extent to which the mood of the soldiers and workers had shifted. They imagined that the crisis would be a rerun of the events of April and July and that the government would again prevail. But the Revolution had progressed too far at this stage to expect any such resolution.

As of the afternoon of October 24, the government's position was extremely precarious. Soldiers at the Peter and Paul Fortress agreed to support the authority of the MRC and an immediate transfer of power to the Petrograd Soviet. This decision assured the insurgents of an unlimited supply of weapons, but more importantly it represented an incalculable psychological victory for the Soviet side. Troops with the primary responsibility for guarding the Winter Palace informed government officials that they would no longer remain at their posts. The radical sailors of the battle cruiser *Aurora* refused their superior's orders to put out to sea and offered their full service to the Soviet. Troops from the MRC took control of the telegraph office at five o'clock without a single shot fired. No additional help from the countryside would be forthcoming either: some units refused outright to come to the government's aid, while others were prevented from marching on the capital by soldiers and workers loyal to the Soviet. The commander of the Petrograd garrison sent a telegram to the supreme commander of the army that read: "I report that the situation in Petrograd is threatening. There are no street outbreaks or disorders, but a systematic seizure of institutions and stations and arrests are going on. No orders are carried out. The cadets surrender their posts without any resistance."

Despite the deepening crisis, Kerensky continued to appraise events with an incomprehensible overconfidence. That evening, he insisted that the government was prepared to crush the left at a moment's notice and announced that he had ordered the arrest of the entire MRC and leading Bolsheviks, even though it must have been apparent by this time that he did not have sufficient troops at his disposal to carry out such orders. Kerensky could count on only 2,000 cadets, 200 officers, and 200 members of the Women's Shock Battalion—a mere fraction of the forces that the MRC could draw upon.

THE OCTOBER REVOLUTION

The evening of October 24 seemed on the surface to be quite like any other. The streets of the capital were quiet; fashionably dressed groups of theatergoers promenaded down the broad avenue of Nevsky Prospekt; the casinos, restaurants, and cabarets conducted a brisk business as usual. There were no demonstrations, no scenes of unrest in any part of the capital. Neither the MRC nor the Bolshevik leadership had given the go-ahead for a full-scale insurrection. Both groups worried about going too far, too fast, especially with the meeting of the national Congress of Soviets just a day away.

The one figure who worried about the danger of excessive caution was Lenin, who had been impatiently biding his time in the weeks since the party had voted for an insurrection. Unlike the leaders of the party or the MRC who appeared reconciled to a gradual overthrow, Lenin still insisted on an immediate armed uprising. Each passing day without decisive action jeopardized the party's prospects for creating a Bolshevik-dominated government, an outcome that he alone among the party leadership saw as an absolute priority. Waiting for the Congress of Soviets to convene might also give the government valuable time to marshal its forces against the left.

Lenin made several requests to the Bolshevik Central Committee asking permission to come to party headquarters, but fearing for his safety, they refused. By late in the evening of October 24, however, the restless Bolshevik could no longer sit by idly while the Revolution he had waited his entire adult life for passed him by. He doffed his familiar wig and cap and, for added disguise, wrapped a bandage around his face as if he were suffering from a horrible toothache. Lenin traveled all the way through the Vyborg district to the Finland Station in an empty streetcar. There was one close call when he narrowly missed being sighted by a roving military patrol, but shortly after midnight, he safely reached the party's headquarters at Smolny.

Lenin immediately cornered several members of the Central Committee and reprimanded them for the horrendous delay in moving the Revolution forward. Lenin's timely intervention once again pushed the party into bolder actions. Within hours of his arrival at Smolny, the MRC went on the offensive. At 2:00 A.M., Red Guards and garrison regiments captured the main power station and shut off all electricity to government buildings. The post office, state bank, and telephone buildings were seized in the early morning, completely isolating the government forces from the outside world.

During the evening, Lenin drafted a manifesto addressed to the "Citizens of Russia" that proclaimed the transfer of political power to the Soviets:

> The Provisional Government has been overthrown. State power has passed into the hands of the organ of the Petrograd Soviet of Workers' and Soldiers' Deputies and the Military Revolutionary Committee, which stands at the head of the Petrograd proletariat and garrison. The cause for which the people have struggled—the immediate proposal of a democratic peace, the elimination of landlord estates, workers' control over production, the creation of a soviet government—the triumph of this cause has been assured. Long live the workers', soldiers' and peasants' revolution!

Pamphlets with Lenin's manifesto were printed and passed out in the tens of thousands in the morning, but the announcement seemed premature given that the government still controlled the Winter Palace.

Kerensky and his ministers spent the early hours of October 25 trying in vain to conjure up the nonexistent forces that would come to the aid of the government. There was no hope of escaping from the trap: one general appraising the situation told the prime minister that the entire Petrograd garrison had gone over to the Bolsheviks. "It is as if the Provisional Government," he said, "were in the capital of an enemy country." Kerensky decided his only hope was to rally troops from the front in person, so just after 10 in the morning, a car bearing the prime minister hurtled through the picket of MRC soldiers surrounding the Winter Palace and sped out of the capital.

The Bolsheviks were determined to grab complete control of the city before the national Congress of Soviets opened, but they failed to press forward their initial advantage. The MRC enjoyed an overwhelming numerical superiority of firepower and troops, and indeed a bold strike early in the morning would have easily captured the Winter Palace from its inexperienced and outnumbered defenders. However, they woefully overestimated the strength of their adversaries and spent the better part of the day fruitlessly awaiting the arrival of reinforcements. The original deadline for the final assault on the government stronghold was 12 noon, yet this was first postponed to 3 o'clock, then to 6, and by dusk, the Winter Palace was still not in the hands of the insurgents. Just after 9:30 P.M., the cruiser *Aurora*, moored in the Neva a short distance away, and the batteries at the Peter and Paul Fortress commenced firing on the palace. Most shells exploded harmlessly in the air but the thunderous reverberations of the artillery unnerved many palace defenders into fleeing their posts.

The Congress of Soviets convened at 10:30 P.M. amid the booming echoes of the attack on the Winter Palace. The attention of all the delegates was riveted on the drama unfolding outside. Speaker after speaker from the moderate socialist parties rose to denounce the action of the Bolsheviks. They demanded that all hostilities should be halted immediately and another coalition government formed to ensure the peace. The moderate socialists decided to walk out of the congress rather than agree to the Bolsheviks' seizure of power. They were soon joined by the left wing of the Mensheviks, who vehemently protested the Bolsheviks' decision to form a new government composed exclusively of Bolshevik representatives rather than a broad socialist coalition. These fateful choices, reflecting both long-held antagonisms and passions that had become inflamed in the furious debate, would prove of lasting importance for the course of the Revolution. By completely repudiating the actions of the Bolsheviks and the workers and soldiers who willingly followed them and by refusing to even debate the makeup of the new regime, these socialist groups made future compromise more difficult and abdicated control over the course of the Revolution to the Bolsheviks.

Well after midnight, when the proceedings inside the Congress of Soviets were reaching their culmination, the MRC readied their forces for a final assault on the Winter Palace. The attack was almost anticlimactic and by no means resembled the heroic storming of the Winter Palace so often depicted in Soviet history books and films. The troops loyal to the government had dwindled considerably throughout the day, leaving only a skeleton force guarding the palace. Entire sections of the building were left unprotected, and Red Guards gradually infiltrated through the lightly guarded areas. There were a few brief skirmishes from time to time, but the MRC units moved in small groups, from floor to floor, disarming some soldiers and persuading others to lay down their arms. Shortly after two in the morning, a frontal assault on the palace overran the last of the resistance and arrested the government ministers.

A NEW WORLD DAWNS

Late in the day of October 26, the members of the new Soviet government were announced before the Congress with Lenin as the chairman of the Council of Peoples' Commissars and Trotsky as commissar of foreign affairs. Lenin appeared at the podium to read out the initial decrees of the Revolutionary government. He began with what he called "the most pressing question of the present day—peace." Lenin read out a "Peace Declaration to Peoples of All the Belligerent Countries," which called upon all nations to begin immediate negotiations for a just, democratic peace, without punitive sanctions or annexations of territory. The Bolsheviks, he insisted, were willing to consider any peace proposal without any preconditions, but henceforth Russia's involvement in this monstrous war was finished.

Lenin then took up the next plank of the Bolshevik platform. Reading from a draft decree on land that he had scribbled on a piece of paper the night before, he declared "the first day of the government of the workers and peasants revolution must be to settle the land

JOHN REED—AMERICAN COMMUNIST

John Reed was an American journalist whose book *Ten Days That Shook the World* is considered to be one of the best eyewitness accounts of the Russian Revolution. Born into America's upper classes, Reed was also one of the founders of the American Communist party, and after his death, his ashes were buried beneath the Kremlin Wall. He was immortalized in the Hollywood movie biography of his life, *Reds*.

Reed was born in Portland, Oregon in 1887. He attended a series of prep schools but because of constant illnesses, grew up as an outsider, with few close friends. At Harvard University, Reed became a compulsive joiner, participating as a football cheerleader, captain of the polo team, managing editor of a campus newspaper, and a member of political clubs.

After graduation in 1910, Reed landed a position as a journalist on the recommendation of Lincoln Steffens, a famous muckraking columnist. He fell in love with the bohemian life of Greenwich Village in New York City, an area that attracted the best and brightest in the arts, literature, and culture. Among his fellow residents were dancer Isadora Duncan, photographer Alfred Stieglitz, anarchist Emma Goldman, and psychoanalyst Sigmund Freud. Reed became the managing editor and political correspondent for *The Masses*, a radical paper devoted to investigative journalism and avant garde art. It was the home for socialists, feminists, anarchists, and anti-establishment figures of all persuasions. Their manifesto read:

> We refuse to commit ourselves to any course of action, except this: to do with *The Masses* exactly what we please . . . Poems, stories, drawings rejected by the capitalistic press on account of their excellence will find a welcome . . . We intend to be arrogant, impertinent, in bad taste, but not vulgar . . . to attack old systems, old morals, old prejudices, . . . bound by no creed or theory of social reform, we will express them all, providing they be radical.

As a reporter, Reed had a boundless energy, a thirst for reckless adventure, and an insatiable desire to expose exploitation and injustice. He traveled throughout the United States, covering the radical movements of the age. He wrote a moving story of a strike by copper workers in Ludlow, Colorado that was crushed by a police massacre in which hundreds of strikers, their wives, and children were killed. He wrote about the strike of textile workers in Paterson, New Jersey that was organized by the Industrial Workers of the World (IWW), a union that was trying to organize all of the unskilled workers. He covered the Mexican Revolution, traveling with Pancho Villa, a charismatic revolutionary leader. Yet, the more Reed wrote about these stirring events, the less satisfied he became with merely being a reporter.

In August 1917, he set sail for Russia: all of his instincts, both journalistic and political, convinced him that he belonged in Russia covering the events unfolding there. His inquisitive nature and boyish enthusiasm served him well in his travels throughout revolutionary Russia with his wife and fellow journalist Louise Bryant. At one trip to the front, he beautifully captured the passion for democratic empowerment that was sweeping the nation:

> The thirst for education, so long thwarted, burst with the Revolution into a frenzy of expression. Russia absorbed reading material like hot sand drinks water, insatiable . . . Lectures, debates, speeches—in theaters, circuses, school-houses, clubs, Soviet meeting rooms, Union headquarters, barracks . . . trenches in the front, in village squares, factories . . . For months in Petrograd, and all over Russia, every street corner was a public tribune . . . We came down to the front of the Twelfth Army, back of Riga, where gaunt and bootless men sickened in the mud of desperate trenches; and when they saw us they started up, with their pinched faces and the flesh showing blue through their torn clothing, demanding eagerly, "Did you bring anything to read?"

In the October Days, Reed seemed to be at every factory meeting, skirmish, street demonstration, or important Soviet meeting. On the day of the storming of the Winter Palace, Reed and several other American journalists managed to sneak into the palace to interview the defending soldiers. Later that evening, he was at the historic meeting of the Soviet when the Bolsheviks announced the formation of a Soviet regime. His marvelous account of the end of that historic occasion is also worth recalling:

> Suddenly, by common impulse, we found ourselves on our feet, mumbling together into the smooth lifting unison of the Internationale. A grizzled old soldier was sobbing like a child. Alexandra Kollontai rapidly winked the tears back. The immense sound rolled through the hall, burst windows and doors and seared into the quiet sky. "The war is ended!" said a young workman near me, his face shining. And when it was over, as we stood there in a kind of awkward hush, someone in the back of the room shouted, "Comrades! Let us remember those who have died for liberty!" So we began to sing the Funeral March, that slow, melancholy and yet triumphant chant, so Russian and so moving . . . The Funeral March seemed the very soul of those dark masses whose delegates sat in this hall, building from their obscure visions a new Russia—and perhaps more.

Reed had been a political radical all his life, but the October Revolution transformed him into a committed revolutionary.

question, which can pacify and satisfy the masses of poor peasants." The Soviet regime was abolishing immediately all private ownership of the land without compensation to the former owners. All lands belonging to the monarchy, church, and landlord estates would be transferred to the peasant communes and then shared out among the individual peasants. Finally, Lenin pledged the Soviet government's support for a system of workers' control and promised to bring the full resources of the state to bear on improving the lives of the Russian working class.

Barely 24 hours after their seizure of power, the Bolsheviks had demonstrated their determination to fulfill their major promises to the people—peace, land, and bread. A new era for Russia and the world was about to dawn.

He returned to the United States, where he toured the country speaking in support of the revolution. Yet the United States was in the grip of the first of the anti-Communist hysterias that were destined to sweep the nation periodically. The Masses was banned and Reed was indicted for sedition. Turning away from journalism to an active commitment to politics, Reed became one of the founders of the American Communist party and returned secretly to Russia in 1919 to present credentials for the new organization to the newly formed Communist International. Russia was not quite the revolutionary paradise that Reed remembered: the specter of hunger and disease as a result of the Civil War, the breakdown of democracy within the Bolshevik party, and the undemocratic tactics of the Bolshevik leaders created considerable disenchantment. Reed attempted to return to the United States but was captured in Finland and imprisoned in horrifying conditions. He was deported back to Russia, where he resumed his duties with the Communist International. After a trip to Baku, Reed contracted typhus and died in Moscow in October 1920, just days before his 33rd birthday.

CHAPTER EIGHT NOTES

p. 96   "All the objective conditions exist . . ." Lenin, quoted in Rabinowitch, p. 180.

p. 98   "Few modern historical episodes . . . ." Rabinowitch, p. 208.

p. 100   "I could pray . . ." Alexander Kerensky, quoted in Chamberlin, pp. 297–298.

p. 100   "The Soviet regime will . . ." Leon Trotsky, quoted in Sukhanov, p. 129.

p. 101   "I report that the situation . . ." Quoted in Chamberlin, p. 315.

p. 103   "The Provisional Government has . . ." Rabinowitch, pp. 274–75.

p. 104   "It is as if . . ." Quoted in Rabinowitch, p. 272.

CHAPTER 9

REVOLUTION
AND CIVIL WAR

The Bolsheviks' seizure of power did not mark the end of the Russian Revolution. The Bolsheviks controlled Petrograd and were victorious in Moscow after a week of brutal fighting, but they still needed to extend their revolutionary control across the vast stretches of the former empire. However, within the first weeks following the Revolution, counterrevolutionary forces had already begun to mobilize armed resistance against the revolutionary government. The political makeup of the revolutionary regime was an open question as well. The Bolsheviks alone had proclaimed a new government, but it was unclear whether the other socialist parties would share in governmental authority or whether a multiparty democracy would flourish. Likewise, the Bolsheviks supposedly had seized power on behalf of the Soviets, but it was unclear how they intended to delegate political power to the popular democratic organizations. These questions would have been extraordinarily complicated even in the most favorable of circumstances, but the Bolshevik government was faced first with a paralyzing economic crisis and then, eight months after the October Revolution, would be thrown into a catastrophic civil war that completely transformed the nature of the revolutionary regime.

THE CONTRADICTIONS OF SOVIET RULE

The makeup of the revolutionary government was shaped by two developments in the aftermath of October. Within a week of the fall of the Winter Palace, the Bolsheviks opened negotiations with the other socialist parties about possible representation in a coalition government, a position that received widespread support within the Bolshevik party. However, compromise proved impossible after the moderate socialists insisted that they would participate in a government only on the condition that both Lenin and Trotsky be barred from serving in any coalition government, a restriction that none of the Bolsheviks were willing to accept. In November, national elections for the Constituent Assembly were held: the Bolsheviks won the urban centers and garrisons by a large majority but captured only 25 percent of the overall vote, well behind the SRs, who took 40 percent. The Bolsheviks decided to ignore these election results: they claimed that their mandate to govern had been confirmed by their overwhelming support among the workers and soldiers who had made the Revolution. Accordingly, when the Constituent Assembly convened on January 18, 1918, Red Guards dismissed the delegates after a single meeting and it was never reopened.

Both decisions profoundly influenced the future of the revolutionary regime. The continued refusal of the moderate socialists to compromise meant that the Bolsheviks were given a free hand to identify the Revolution as their exclusive province and this undoubtedly colored their attitudes toward the Constituent Assembly. Nevertheless, the Bolshevik's flagrant disregard for democratic procedures left them in a damning contradiction: they presumably owed their mandate for power to their popularity among the masses, but it was unclear whether they would be prepared to surrender political power should their own support among the revolutionary constituency of 1917 ever falter.

The relationship between the popular democratic organizations and the Bolshevik-dominated central government was equally complex. The Bolsheviks had previously insisted that a Soviet regime would be qualitatively more democratic than the representative systems of liberal democracy in the West. In the Soviet system, citizens would enjoy the power to recall their representatives at any time and not merely at regular intervals. In the Soviet system, citizens would be empowered to take an active role in the daily administration of the government. In the Soviet system, politics would no longer be the exclusive preserve of educated elites but would be placed within the reach of ordinary men and women. "We shall find that we can teach the vast masses of workers to administer the state and industry," Lenin wrote, "to develop practical skills, to overcome the noxious, age old prejudice that the administration of the state is the business of privileged men." Soviet power promised practical advantages as well: only the popular organizations, by galvanizing the initiative of millions of citizens, could stave off an impending social and economic catastrophe.

Indeed, in the first months after the Revolution, the organizations of the revolutionary democracy established popular control over an ever-increasing scope of Russian political life. Soviets set up day-care centers, continuing education programs, and resettlement offices for returning veterans. They coordinated communal housing, poor relief, and orphan care. Factory committees took an active role in economic affairs, organizing the food supply, locating scarce fuel and raw materials, coordinating job centers, finding funds to pay workers, and securing new orders for production. The Soviets and factory committees enjoyed considerable autonomy from the central government in implementing policy and were far from being a rubber stamp for the wishes of the Bolshevik leaders.

However, this system of revolutionary democracy eventually began to unravel. It became extremely difficult to find sufficiently motivated and qualified people to help the Soviets or factory committees meet their expanding obligations. The most talented workers were sent to consolidate the Revolution in the provinces, or found important posts in the government or party, or were recruited to the newly formed Red Army. As the excitement of the revolutionary period began to ebb, there were fewer and fewer ideologically committed workers who were willing to spend the huge amounts of spare time that participation in the popular organizations necessitated.

These difficulties were further exacerbated by the onset of economic crisis. In the aftermath of the October Revolution, the Russian economy suffered a calamity on the scale of a modern Black Death. The Bolsheviks' immediate ending of Russia's participation in the war wreaked havoc on the economy: the vast majority of industries, which were involved in defense production, ground to a halt overnight, and within six months, output had contracted to 19th-century levels and unemployment had skyrocketed to over 60 percent of the work force. The largely uncoordinated demobilization of millions of soldiers, who returned to their former work places demanding their old jobs back, only exacerbated the pressures on all workers.

The crisis in industry aggravated a crisis in agriculture. After the Bolshevik land reform, the Russian countryside was transformed into an ocean of small family farms, oriented toward family consumption, not production for the market. There was little incentive for peasants to develop either innovative production techniques or higher levels of agricultural output, because there were no manufactured products available that they could buy in exchange for their crops. The overall result was a sharp decline in agricultural production and consequently a precipitous drop in the food supply in Russia's urban centers.

The mood of the workers changed sharply. The enthusiasm and exhilaration of the early months of the regime were transformed into barely concealed panic. The specter of starvation, uncertainty, and insecurity gripped everyone. Many were forced to resort to pilfering and theft at their work places to stay alive; others joined the Red Army seeking greater security; hundreds of thousands returned to their ancestral villages in search of relief from the unending hardship. This economic catastrophe had profound consequences for the revolutionary democracy. With so many people preoccupied with eking out their daily survival, the incentive to participate in the popular organizations became harder and harder to sustain. Workers' faith in the benefits of democratic control was likewise undermined: factory committees were not able to solve the problems of a declining food supply or mushrooming unemployment, nor could the Soviets help provide greater economic security. Under such extreme conditions, the Bolshevik leadership, with the encouragement of many workers, believed that only strong governmental control over economic and political life could avert a disaster, but no one knew how this could be accomplished while at the same time maintaining the traditions of grass roots democracy. There were no easy answers to this dilemma, and before a resolution could be reached in a democratic manner, the country was engulfed in a divisive civil war.

THE ORDEAL OF CIVIL WAR

The Russian Civil War was a protracted national agony, a pitiless struggle marked by extraordinary suffering, cruelty, and hardship. In a desperate effort to survive against crushing odds, the Communist (as the Bolsheviks became known) government waged war for nearly three years, across the entire reach of its 5,000 mile territory, against a variety of armies, which had the support of more than a dozen foreign powers, including the United States, Great Britain, France, Germany, and Japan. The Civil War was not just a military conflict, but a continuation of the revolutionary process itself. The conflict was seen, not just in Russia but internationally as well, as a war of principles, a battle between two opposing classes with competing political visions and programs. The Russian Civil War, like all such conflicts, had to be contested not simply by virtue of superior military force but by political programs as well; military victory in a civil war would be shortlived unless it could be backed up by political power.

The war broke out in the early summer of 1918, just a few months after the Bolsheviks had signed a peace treaty with Germany. The counterrevolutionaries (known as Whites), although divided between monarchists, liberals, and right-wing socialists, were nevertheless united in their desire to overthrow the revolutionary (Red) regime. White armies were mobilized and quickly threatened the Soviet republic from the north, south, and east. Because the White armies fought over such a large territory, their forces had to operate independently of each other and without any central coordination. However, the Whites could count on one huge advantage that the Bolsheviks were unable to match: the full military and material support of the Allied powers.

The Western democracies provided ample funds and supplies for the White armies and imposed an economic blockade against the Soviet republic that starved it of all financial credit and goods from the West. They adamantly refused to extend diplomatic recognition to the new Soviet government, yet they were willing to establish relations with any White government that was formed, no matter how short-lived or repressive. They sent over 180,000 troops to fight alongside the White armies: the British landed troops in Archangel and Murmansk, the Americans and Japanese in the Far East and Siberia, the French in the

Staff of the American expeditionary army, which invaded Russia during the Russian Civil War (National Archives)

Ukraine and the Caucasus. The Allied intervention was a willful flouting of international law and a callous disregard of Russian sovereignty, yet the Allies tried to justify their actions by arguing that "bolshevism," in the words of the British prime minister Lloyd George, was a "menace to civilization."

Against these formidable adversaries, the revolutionary government entrusted the defense of the revolution to the Red Army. Given the disintegration of the old army, the Bolsheviks were forced to build an entire new military force from scratch. This momentous task was entrusted to Trotsky, who became commissar of war in the spring of 1918. The core of the Red Army was made up of Red Guards and devoted party recruits who formed the crack battalions, but at the height of the war, the army contained more than 5 million soldiers, most of whom were peasants conscripted into service through a compulsory draft. The Red Army was organized along conventional hierarchical lines, with soldiers subject to harsh military discipline and officers appointed from the top rather than elected by the troops themselves. Trotsky controversially reinstated old officers from the tsarist army whose professional expertise he felt would be invaluable in such a conflict. To ensure the officers followed orders, he paired each officer with a political commissar who had to countersign every order and shared responsibility for battlefield strategy. To ensure the officers' loyalty, he had their families taken hostage and ordered them to be executed in case the officers deserted or behaved duplicitously.

Indeed, terror became a hallmark of both the Red and White sides. In every town or city they captured, White armies rounded up workers, suspected Bolshevik sympathizers, and members of the Jewish population for mass executions. Peasant villages that offered support to the Red Army were put to the torch and all of its citizens killed by a firing squad. The Communist government formed the All Russian Extraordinary Commission for Combating Counterrevolution and Sabotage, colloquially known as the Cheka, to organize the Red terror. It arrested and imprisoned thousands in horrifying jails that became sites for brutal interrogations and tortures. It executed thousands of prisoners without trials, among them the tsar and his entire family, who were killed in July 1918. In areas under Red control hostages were randomly seized and killed in reprisal for White terror. The Cheka similarly engaged in collective punishment of their so-called class enemies: people were arrested and executed not because of their actual or suspected guilt but because of their social origins, education, or political ideology. The Cheka conducted its summary justice outside the normal channels of politics with no oversight and without any concern for legal procedures. The rights of the accused to an attorney or trial were routinely ignored, so people were mistakenly sent to their deaths on numerous occasions. All told, more than 100,000 civilians lost their lives in the heat of the Civil War.

These policies of terror were not entirely unexpected: one of the hallmarks of all civil wars is the way in which they elicit extremes of emotion, such as hatred, despair, and a desire for vengeance. When two sides are locked in mortal combat, and both know full well that should their opponents win they will be given no quarter, terror is inevitable. Yet, it is also true that the Bolsheviks, as revolutionaries who promised the creation of a more democratic and just society, had a special responsibility to make a conscious effort to maintain the greatest possible consistency between the goals of the Revolution and the methods employed to safeguard it. However, there were no attempts

The tsar was imprisoned after the Revolution. He and his family were executed during the Civil War in July 1918. (National Archives)

made to restrict the Cheka's unlimited powers or to provide legal safeguards whereby the accused would be granted the right to an attorney and an open trial before worker tribunals. The Red terror became a tragic mistake on the part of the Bolsheviks: it was no surprise that the one institution that emerged relatively unscathed through the

A HISTORY OF THE RUSSIAN REVOLUTION

Civil War was the secret police, which became a permanent feature of the Soviet state.

While terror scarred the political landscape, the Civil War devastated the economy and brought unbelievable hardship to the entire Russian population. With industry in virtual collapse, the Communist regime launched a radical restructuring of the economy, known as "war communism," that abolished private property, nationalized all businesses, and outlawed free trade. The government sent armed detachments of workers and soldiers into the countryside to obtain surplus produce from the peasants in order to guarantee enough food for the cities and the Red Army. Though these units were instructed to leave the peasants enough for their personal needs, they typically took grain that was in fact part of the peasants own meager supply.

The peasants violently resisted these armed bands and, more importantly, drastically reduced their production to mere subsistence levels. As a result, it became next to impossible to live in Russia's cities: official food rations were minute and the only way to eat was to barter for food on the black market. The weakest elements of society—the sick, the elderly, and the young—were the least able to bargain for food and suffered desperately. Heating fuel was in short supply, so people burned books and furniture to keep warm. Tens of thousands of workers abandoned the cities to return to their former peasant villages in search of food and greater economic security. The spread of typhus and other diseases took a dreadful toll on the urban population, and a horrifying famine spread throughout the countryside killing millions in its wake.

Amid such devastation, the Red and White armies engaged in a fierce tug of war across all of Russia, with fortunes switching back and forth every month. At one time the Whites controlled the entire Ukraine and most of Siberia, threatened the Urals, and came within nine miles of seizing Petrograd. Red Army counterattacks successfully drove back each White offensive, and by the spring of 1920, the Bolsheviks, against all odds, were able to achieve a victory that guaranteed the continued existence of the regime. Their triumph was the combination of their own political and military skills and the ineptitude of their opponents. The Bolsheviks created a powerful war machine that reflected the brilliant, charismatic leadership of Lenin and Trotsky

Russian Civil War, 1918–1920

Barents Sea

SWEDEN

St.Petersburg

1917
February Revolution—
Tsar Nicholas II abdicates;
provisional government
established.
October Revolution—
Bolsheviks under Vladimir
Lenin seize power.

FINLAND

Ekaterinburg

July 1918
Tsar Nicholas II and family
executed by Bolsheviks.

Baltic
Sea

ESTONIA

St. Petersburg

Ekaterinburg

Moscow

January 1918
Bolsheviks move
government
from St. Petersburg.

LITHUANIA

LATVIA

GERMANY
(Danzig)

Moscow

B O L S H E V I K   R U S S I A

Warsaw

Minsk

Omsk →

POLAND

Orenburg

CZECHOSLOVAKIA

Kiev

HUNGARY

UKRAINE

ROMANIA

BULGARIA

Black Sea

Caspian Sea

GEORGIA

ARMENIA

AZERBAIJAN

Aegean
Sea

TURKEY

PERSIA

──────── Boundary of Russian Empire, 1914   ─ ─ ─ ─ Boundary of Soviet Union, 1922

Area controlled by the Bolshevik
(communist) government by
October 1919

Date independence recognized
by the Soviet Union

Fighting between Red (Bolshevik)
and White (anti-Bolshevik) armies

This map shows areas of major action during the 1917 Revolution and the Civil War.

and the presence of an effective, idealistically committed party network. The White governments were ineffective, corrupt regimes that remained the preserve of arbritary despots. While the Bolsheviks may have been despised by many peasants, this did not come close to matching the hatred and fear the peasants felt for the old political order that the Whites so conspicuously represented. The Soviet regime represented a revolution in the land that seemed irreversible: the Whites could only herald a return to the dreaded past. It was no surprise then that the peasants saw the Bolsheviks as the lesser of two evils and sided with them against the Whites.

The Bolshevik's victory was won at a horrifying cost. Casualties in the Red Army during the war totalled 1.5 million, a figure equaled by the White forces. These figures were dwarfed by the deaths from hunger and epidemics that swept over Russia in the Civil War years. All told, probably nine million Russians lost their lives as a result of the Civil War.

THE SHATTERED DREAMS OF 1917

The disastrous evolution of the Russian Revolution can ultimately be attributed to the devastating impact of the Civil War. No aspect of Russian politics or society was left untouched by these horrendous years. First, the Civil War brought about a massive reshaping of the social landscape of Russia. The old elites from the aristocracy and bourgeoisie were either eliminated by the Red terror or emigrated to the West during the war years. The heroic proletariat that had propelled the Revolution forward, and in whose name the Bolsheviks had taken power, virtually disappeared: the populations of Petrograd and Moscow, which numbered nearly four million in 1917, were reduced to 1.4 million by 1921. The peasantry weathered the storm of war far better than other social groups: their percentage of the total population increased dramatically, and agriculture once again became the nation's most important economic asset. None of these developments were favorable for a government that hoped to create a modern, industrialized, socialist society.

The Civil War marked the complete political transformation of the Revolution. The rich fabric of Soviet democracy was utterly lost: the financial and organizational resources previously devoted to the revolutionary democracy were allocated to the war effort and the demo-

THE RUSSIAN REVOLUTION IN THE WORLD

Internationalism was a motivating spirit of many political ideologies of the early 20th century. Liberals envisioned a world of self-determination for all men and women, such as that articulated by President Woodrow Wilson in his historic Fourteen Points. All Russian revolutionaries, Mensheviks and Bolsheviks alike, were convinced that they were living at the dawn of a new socialist epoch. They believed that a revolution in Russia, the weakest link in the international system, would inevitably spark further revolutions that would sweep across Europe.

Indeed, it was a deeply held belief among most Bolsheviks that the Russian Revolution could not possibly survive unless revolution spread to the most advanced capitalist countries. A manifesto of the Kronstadt sailors read: "The future of the Russian Revolution, we are sure, will spread over the world and light a fire in the hearts of the workers of all lands, and we shall obtain support in our struggle. . . ." "We place all our hopes," said Trotsky before the Congress of Soviets in October 1917, "in the fact that our revolution will trigger a European revolution. If the people of Europe do not rise up and crush imperialism, we will be crushed."

As we now know, the Bolsheviks seriously overestimated the political attraction of a socialist revolution for the workers of Europe and underestimated the resiliency of capitalist democracies to weather their revolutionary challenge. Yet, in the aftermath of the October Revolution, the Bolshevik's confidence did not appear misplaced. The Revolution unleashed a wave of revolutionary movements across Western Europe and Asia. Two million workers in Italy went on strike in 1920; the strike culminated in a wave of factory occupations and seizures of landlord estates that stopped just short of an insurrection. A year earlier in Germany, the Spartacist uprising, which attempted the overthrow of the new German republic, ended in dismal failure and its leaders, Rosa Luxemburg and Karl Liebknecht, were assassinated; a second revolutionary upsurge

Demonstration in Budapest celebrating the Hungarian Revolution
(National Archives)

in 1923 was also crushed. A revolutionary regime was established in Hungary in 1919, but it too was shortlived, lasting only four months before being brutally repressed by a counterrevolutionary force. Although none of the uprisings in this period proved successful, the Russian Revolution continued to exert tremendous appeal to radicals around the world for years to come. In the following decades the revolutions in China, Vietnam, and Cuba drew much of their inspiration from the Bolsheviks' example.

The Russian Revolution's impact on America was equally profound. It colored American domestic politics and foreign policy making for nearly 70 years. American radicals who had anything favorable to say about the Revolution were denounced for being anti-American. In the first episode of "Redbaiting" in American history, the Palmer Raids in 1919 launched a vicious attack on the American left: antiwar activists were imprisoned, socialist parties and newspapers were banned, radicals were deported for holding rallies or speaking in public, travelers from Russia were investigated by the FBI. In the 1950s, a similar anti-Communist crusade was begun by Senator Joseph McCarthy: televised congressional hearings created a nationwide hysteria that resulted in members of the American Communist party, and many just suspected of being communist sympathizers, being fired from their jobs, refused the right to vote, and blacklisted from employment in universities, newspapers, and Hollywood.

Anti-communism was to have profoundly harmful effects on American politics. Such a climate of suspicion, in which any progressive belief or any opposition to government policy could be branded as "anti-American," was bound to exert a chilling effect on all forms of dissent. It represented a perversion of the Constitution's guarantee of free speech for all Americans no matter what their views. This anti-Communist hysteria affected American foreign policy as well. For years, the American government saw fit to interpret any opposition to its policies or supporters abroad as evidence of a communist conspiracy. Democratically elected left-wing regimes, such as those in the Dominican Republic, Chile, and Guatemala, were overthrown with the active assistance of the American government because of this anti-Communist mentality. Likewise, the nation's long and costly war in Vietnam, a war that left more than 50,000 Americans and one million Vietnamese dead, was the direct result of the government's unwillingness to accept the establishment of a popularly supported Communist regime in that country.

cratic decision-making of the Soviets was bypassed because wartime circumstances required the sort of quick, authoritative decision-making that only a strong central government could manage. Over time, the Soviets and factory committees became entirely powerless, with no meaningful check on the central government. Yet, the Bolsheviks made no special attempt to revive the institutions of democracy once the crisis had passed: the abolition of Soviet democracy was never repudiated within the party or viewed as a horrible defeat for the Revolution.

Despite all their professed commitments to the revolutionary democracy in 1917, the Bolsheviks never accepted the Soviets and factory committees as indispensable elements of a socialist government or attempted to formulate how they could contribute to the Revolution in any constructive way. Even though revolutionary Russia would one day be renamed the Soviet Union, the "Soviet" character of the regime remained entirely fictitious.

The Civil War marked the demise of democracy within the Communist party as well. The Bolsheviks had previously enjoyed a rich and turbulent political life: there was a great diversity of opinion within the party and party leaders were often publicly challenged and criticized. Indeed, all the major issues facing the party during the Revolution and the first year of the Soviet regime were vigorously debated at all levels of the party. Yet this vital democracy soon disappeared under the pressures of civil war. The primary decision-making authority became the province of the party's five-man executive, the Politburo; other party forums, such as the party congresses, became little more than rubber stamps for decisions made by this tiny elite. Opposition groups within the party were outlawed in 1921; although this ban on factions was supposed to be a temporary measure that would be rescinded once the political and economic circumstances had improved, it too became a permanent feature.

The abandonment of internal party democracy coincided with the decline of democracy in everyday political life. In Soviet elections held immediately before the Civil War broke out, the Bolsheviks had already begun to lose ground among the working class, losing their majority to the Mensheviks and SRs, and at war's end, their popularity among their former supporters was considerably less than that of their political rivals. Yet, the Bolsheviks were unwilling to tolerate any form of democratic dissent or challenge to their rule. All political parties, except the Communist party, were outlawed and all civil liberties were eliminated. The Communists' monopoly of political power, even after the crisis of the Civil War had receded, made a mockery of their professed commitment to proletarian democracy. Rosa Luxemburg, a German revolutionary, criticized the Bolsheviks' repression of political freedom:

Freedom only for the supporters of the government, only for the members of one party—however numerous they may be—is no freedom at all. Freedom is always and exclusively freedom for the one who thinks differently. Not because of any fanatical concept of justice, but because all that is instructive, wholesome and purifying in political freedom depends upon this essential characteristic and its effectiveness vanishes when freedom becomes a special privilege.

After the Civil War, it would have been possible to provide sufficient political space to restore civil liberties or enable other left-wing parties to participate in the political process, yet the Communist party leadership had evolved to the point where it would not, as a matter of political conviction, consider giving up its absolute control of political power.

The culmination of the Civil War then revealed a stark picture. The economy was in ruins, the proletariat in headlong retreat, the population reduced to physical and psychological exhaustion, the revolutionary democracy dissolved into authoritarianism. The events of 1917 appeared to have faded into distant memory, but there was one last reminder of those stirring moments to come. On March 1, 1921, sailors at Kronstadt seized the island fortress to demand "land and bread," a return to Soviet democracy, and a government without the Bolsheviks. Above all, they wanted to return to the values and aspirations of 1917, yet the Bolshevik party had come a long way from those days of revolution. The Communists now saw their own survival and maintenance of power as the primary objective of the Revolution and to preserve this power, they sent the Red Army to brutally crush the Kronstadt revolt. And in so doing, they laid to rest the revolutionary dreams of 1917.

CHAPTER NINE NOTES

p. 113   "We shall find that we . . ." Lenin, quoted in Liebman, p. 333.

p. 126   "Freedom only for the supporters . . ." Rosa Luxemburg. *The Russian Revolution* (Ann Arbor: University of Michigan Press, 1977), p. 23.

The founder of the Soviet state, Vladimir Lenin, died on January 10, 1924. Weakened by a 1918 assassination attempt, overworked, and afflicted with persistent migraines, Lenin's health had deteriorated throughout the Civil War. In May 1922, he suffered a stroke that left him partly paralyzed and unable to speak or write, yet through intensive therapy and sheer willpower, Lenin regained sufficient strength to begin working again. In a series of articles, he warned of the dangers of authoritarianism and bureaucracy that were distorting the revolutionary state, and on December 25, 1922, he dictated a political testament that highlighted the growing power of Joseph Stalin, the general secretary of the Communist party. Indeed, Lenin suggested that Stalin should be removed from that office. However, shortly afterward, Lenin suffered two more strokes that effectively left him no political influence. Two years later, before any of his proposed reforms could be implemented, he died of a massive brain hemorrage.

March in honor of Lenin's death in 1924 (National Archives)

Lenin's death unleashed a vast outpouring of public sorrow. Hundreds of thousands of Muscovites braved the freezing weather to wait on line for a chance to pay their last respects to Lenin, whose body lay in state for three days. Millions of onlookers crowded the city streets to catch a glimpse of his casket being escorted though the capital by members of the party's Central Committee. The party leadership overruled Lenin's wishes to be buried in a simple grave and instead had his body embalmed and placed behind a glass display case in a grandiose mausoleum specially constructed on Red Square, where it became a site of pilgrimage for decades afterward. In one final tribute, the city of Petrograd, whose name had been changed from St. Petersburg during World War I, was now renamed Leningrad. It would remain so for nearly 70 years: it was only after the collapse of the Communist system in 1991 that the people of the city voted to return it to its original prerevolutionary name of St. Petersburg. Plans are also underway to dismantle the immense mausoleum and give Lenin's body a proper burial in a public cemetery in Moscow.

This ironic turnaround aptly captures the extraordinary evolution of the Soviet political system and society in those intervening years, a transformation that represented the continued destruction, indeed the perversion, of the dreams of 1917. The years after Lenin's death were marked by a bitter political struggle over who would succeed the Bolshevik leader. Stalin, utilizing his control of the party bureaucracy, defeated all of his party opponents by the end of the decade and went on to rule the Soviet Union as an absolute dictator until his death at age 73 in 1953.

The first defining moment of the Stalinist dictatorship began in 1929 when Stalin abruptly reversed the Communist party's policy of actively promoting small-scale private farming in favor of the forced collectivization of Russia's peasantry. Collectivization, whereby all peasants were herded onto state-run collective farms, was a virtual civil war against Russia's 125 million peasants: it destroyed the traditional life and culture of the Russian countryside and precipitated a horrifying famine in 1932–33 that left millions dead. While the countryside was being ravaged, Stalin launched a breakneck industrialization program, known as the Five Year Plan, that wiped out the last vestiges of a private market economy in Russia in favor of a centrally planned economy.

Both programs were dependent on unremittingly brutal terror. Peasants who resisted were executed or perished in the nightmarish conditions of the gulags—prison camps of forced labor that were established in the coldest, most inhospitable parts of Russia. Workers toiled in virtual slave labor conditions and millions of innocent people were arrested, tortured, and disappeared in Stalin's prisons.

Perhaps as many as 20 million people lost their lives in Stalin's holocaust, a figure that does not include the millions of deaths that resulted from his negligent military leadership at the beginning of World War II. Stalin's brutalization of the general population was matched by an extraordinary program of terror directed against the Communist party itself. In a series of show trials (trials in which the verdicts are rigged) between 1936 and 1939, Stalin decimated the ranks of the party leaders who originally built up the party, and massacred several million of the party bureaucracy, military leadership, and intellectuals.

The Stalinist model of totalitarian dictatorship and planned economy was adopted throughout the countries of Eastern Europe—Poland, Czechoslovakia, Hungary, Rumania, Bulgaria, and East Germany were all incorporated after World War II into what became known as the "Soviet bloc"—and indeed persisted in the Soviet Union even after Stalin's death. There was a brief thaw from 1956 to 1962 under the leadership of Nikita Khrushchev. He implemented reforms that released millions of prisoners from the gulags, dismantled the system of police terror, allowed some limited dissent and the publication of anti-Stalinist writings, and publicly disclosed for the first time the full extent of Stalin's responsibility for the genocide. Khrushchev's reforms, however, did not attempt to introduce democracy into either the Communist party or public life, and there was no attempt to change the fundamental inadequacies of the Stalinist economic system. Khrushchev was overthrown in a coup in 1964 and his successors, Leonid Brezhnev, Yuri Andropov, and Constantin Chernenko, defended the Stalinist heritage. They arrested thousands of dissenters, outlawed all criticism of Stalin, and crushed all dissent in the Soviet Union and the Soviet bloc: in 1968, Soviet tanks rolled into Czechoslovakia to crush a political movement for democratic reform known as the Prague Spring.

When Mikhail Gorbachev was named general secretary of the Communist party in March 1985, the Stalinist system had been in a deep crisis for decades. The Soviet Union was a formidable military power yet it was plagued by an ailing economy: the country was far behind its more technologically innovative capitalist rivals in the West in terms of industrial production, and because its agricultural system was incapable of increasing productivity, the country was forced to import millions of pounds of grain each year just to feed its population. This disastrous economic performance, coupled with continued political repression, created widespread dissatisfaction with the regime. On the day he became leader of the Soviet Union, Gorbachev told his wife, Raisa, "We can't go on living like this." He launched an ambitious program of political and economic reform that became one of the most dramatic periods of change in Soviet, if not Russian, history: a reform that would end in the demise of the Communist system and the disintegration of the Soviet Union itself.

Gorbachev's program encompassed a plan of economic restructuring (known as *perestroika*) and political openness (known as *glasnost*) that was intended to create a pluralistic, democratic society with a mixed economy. Comprehensive economic reform was implemented to eliminate central party control of the economy; individual firms and managers were given permission to attract foreign investment or trade directly abroad, and the collective farms were freed to produce and trade on an open market. Gorbachev permitted a greater freedom of expression than ever before: books, previously taboo, that called into question the very foundation of the Soviet system, were allowed to be published and public meetings critical of the regime were allowed to meet unmolested. Even more dramatic, Gorbachev instituted free elections to a newly created national parliament, regional parliaments, and the position of state president. The elections in March 1989 turned out to be a disastrous humiliation for the Communist party; although Gorbachev was elected president, many party candidates were soundly defeated. A year later, the party's constitutional monopoly of power over the political system and the economy was eliminated and supreme authority was transferred to the position of state president, held by Gorbachev. These dramatic changes in the Soviet Union helped pave the way for similar changes throughout the nations of Eastern Europe:

from 1988 onward, these states began abandoning the Communist system in favor of free elections and a mixed economy, a process that culminated with the fall of the Berlin Wall in November 1989 and the reunification of Germany a year later.

To achieve such extraordinary reforms, Gorbachev was forced to maintain a delicate balancing act between conservatives within the Communist party who believed he was moving too fast and those outside who believed he was moving too slowly. It was only a matter of time before his conservative opponents made a move against him. On August 18, 1991, hardliners within the party, the Soviet army, and the KGB (secret police) joined forces in a coup to overthrow Gorbachev and put an end to his reforms. Gorbachev was placed under house arrest at his vacation home in the Crimea, and all communications were severed with the outside world. The leaders of the coup appeared on national television, a broadcast that was seen throughout the world, to announce a state of emergency and proclaim their control of the government on the grounds that Gorbachev was temporarily ill. Yet, the coup collapsed within a mere three days: the resistance in Moscow, led by the president of the Russian Republic, Boris Yeltsin, played a critical role, as did the ineptitude of the plotters. Several hundred thousand protestors gathered at the Russian parliament building (popularly known as the White House), constructed makeshift barricades of overturned buses and scrap metal, and refused to accept the authority of the coup leaders. The conspirators meanwhile were guilty of the most elementary mistakes: they failed to seal off the White House before the Yeltsin supporters arrived, they failed to cut off communications to the outside world, they failed to close down the airports, or to gain the necessary military support for the coup. In the aftermath of the coup, Gorbachev was restored to the presidency, but his power and prestige would never be the same. The Communist party was outlawed and by the end of the year the Soviet Union itself was dissolved and replaced by a loosely affiliated Commonwealth of Independent States. Gorbachev resigned his now defunct post of president of the Soviet Union and uncontested political power within Russia was held by Yeltsin, the president of the Russian Republic, the largest and strongest of the independent states.

The new post-Communist government, as in other periods of Russian history, was faced with the momentous task of rebuilding an economy in the midst of a deepening economic crisis and of establishing the foundations of a democratic system in a country with little memory or sustained experience of democracy. Yeltsin's solution to the economic problem has been to encourage the wholesale privatization of the Russian economy, selling off all state businesses to the private sector and radically reducing the government's control of the economy. Unfortunately, the experiment of transforming Russia into a dynamic capitalist economy has been a dismal failure. Unemployment is now approaching nearly 50 percent of the population, shortages of goods and services are rampant, which has led to corruption on a massive scale and the growing influence of organized crime in everyday life. Inequalities of wealth have become widespread: half the country lives in desperate poverty, while a small number have enriched themselves and become millionaires. Russia is now an extraordinarily polarized society and a resurgence of ethnic hatreds and rivalries threatens to split the entire society wide open.

The creation of a democratic system has also been thwarted. Freedom of the press and airwaves was established, as was a freely elected parliament, but the influence of both has been drastically curtailed by the actions of Yeltsin, who has proved to be another in a long line of authoritarian Russian leaders. Yeltsin has suspended the courts, cracked down on opposition party newspapers, and issued decrees without the consent of the Russian parliament, which opposed his catastrophic economic reforms, inability to compromise, and authoritarian mentality. This contempt for democratic procedures reached its peak in October 1993 when Yeltsin provoked a near civil war by ordering army tanks to open fire against the parliament building after delegates had refused to bow to his demands. The irony was considerable given that only two years earlier it was Yeltsin himself who had stood on a tank outside the White House in defiance of the coup leaders and passionately warned of the consequences for Russian democracy should the army fire on its own citizens. By the end of 1994, Yeltsin had further involved the Russian army in an unpopular war against the Chechen Republic, which threatened to not only bankrupt the Russian government but embroil it in an unending guerrilla war that might provoke prolonged resistance in other republics.

Yeltsin's "October Revolution" eerily recalled echoes of the past, stirring memories of the tsar's dismissal of the Duma in 1906 and the Bolsheviks' dismissal of the Constituent Assembly in 1918. It appears that the fateful lesson of Russian history in the 20th century is that all attempts to build a democratic society end in failure. One can only hope that the lessons of the 21st century will tell a different story.

CHRONOLOGY

May 14, 1894	• Nicholas II crowned tsar of Russia
July 1903	• The Russian Social Democratic party splits into Bolshevik and Menshevik factions
January 22, 1905	• Bloody Sunday: protestors against the tsarist government are massacred by the police, sparking the Revolution of 1905
August 2, 1914	• Russia enters World War I
February 23, 1917	• The February Revolution begins with protests in Petrograd on International Women's Day
February 24	• 200,000 workers strike in Petrograd
February 25	• General strike spreads the rebellion through the capital
February 26	• The revolt continues to escalate
February 27	• Mutiny of the Petrograd garrison. First meeting of the Soviet of Workers' and Soldiers' Deputies. Provisional Committee of the Duma formed
February 28	• Final collapse of Tsarist government
March 2	• Tsar Nicholas II abdicates. Provisional Government created

April 3 • Vladimir Lenin, leader of the Bolsheviks, returns to Russia

April 4 • Lenin discloses his April Theses: the view that the Revolution must continue against the Provisional Government

April 18 • Provisional Government affirms its intentions to continue the war to victory

April 20–21 • April Days: massive demonstrations in Petrograd against the government's war policy. New Provisional Government formed, a coalition between liberals and moderate socialists

May 4 • Trotsky arrives from America and announces support for the Bolsheviks

June 16 • Kerensky, minister of war, orders a new Russian offensive

July 3–5 • July Days: mass demonstrations against the coalition by Bolskevik-inspired workers and soldiers stops short of an insurrection. Bolsheviks arrested and Lenin goes into hiding in Finland

August 28 • General Kornilov launches a military coup against the revolutionary leadership but is stopped by the resistance of the Petrograd workers and his own troops

September 9 • The Bolsheviks acquire a majority in the Petrograd Soviet

October 10 • Lenin's proposal for an armed insurrection against the Provisional Government is adopted by the Bolshevik party

October 21 • The Military Revolutionary Committee, created by the Petrograd Soviet, establishes authority over the Petrograd garrison

October 25 • October Revolution begins. Insurgents capture strategic points around the capital. Kerensky flees the Winter Palace. Bolsheviks declare the Provisional Government overthrown and proclaim Soviet regime

October 26 •	Winter Palace falls to the Bolshevik forces. Second All Russian Congress of Soviets passes decrees on peace and land reform. The Council of Peoples Commissars established
March 3, 1918 •	Brest Litovsk treaty between Russia and Germany signed. Russian involvement in World War I ends
June 1918 •	Russian Civil War begins
June 1920 •	Last of the White armies is defeated. Civil War ends
March 1, 1921 •	Sailors of the Kronstadt fortress revolt against the Communist regime

BIBLIOGRAPHY AND
FURTHER READING

GENERAL HISTORIES

Chamberlin, William, *The Russian Revolution, 1917–1921* (New York: Macmillan, 1935). 2 vols. One of the earliest historical accounts of the Revolution and still one of the finest.

Cohen, Stephen F., *Rethinking the Soviet Experience* (New York and Oxford: Oxford University Press, 1985). An outstanding scholarly book that provides an alternative account of Soviet history from 1917 until the early 1980s.

Liebman, Marcel, *The Russian Revolution* (New York: Vintage, 1970). A fine general history.

Pipes, Richard, *The Russian Revolution 1899–1919* (New York: Knopf, 1990). A well-written restatement of the traditional historical writing of the Revolution.

Trotsky, Leon, *The History of the Russian Revolution* (London: Pluto Press, 1977). Classic text, originally written in 1932, is a partisan, sometimes biased account, yet remains a marvelously written and stirring history.

ABOUT THE REVOLUTION

Farber, Samuel, *Before Stalinism: The Rise and Fall of Soviet Democracy* (London and New York: Verso, 1990). A scholarly but readable account of when and why the Russian Revolution began to go wrong.

Ferro, Marc, *October 1917: A Social History of the Russian Revolution* (London: Routledge, 1980). Interesting look at how the Revolution transformed the lives of ordinary Russians.

Lincoln, Bruce, *Red Victory* (New York: Simon and Schuster, 1990). A panoramic history of the Russian Civil War, especially strong on the military campaigns.

Rabinowitch, Alexander, *The Bolsheviks Come to Power: The Revolution of 1917 in Petrograd* (New York: Norton, 1978). An important academic text that served as a useful corrective to the standard account of the Bolshevik's rise to power.

Smith, S. A., *Red Petrograd: Revolution in the Factories 1917–1918* (Cambridge: Cambridge University Press, 1983). A compelling scholarly account of how the Revolution dramatically reshaped the fortunes of the Petrograd workers.

MEMOIRS AND BIOGRAPHIES

Deutscher, Isaac, *The Prophet Armed: Trotsky: 1879–1921* (New York: Vintage, 1965). A brilliant biography of the Bolshevik leader.

Haney, John, *Vladimir Lenin* (New York: Chelsea House, 1988). An excellent introductory biography.

Reed, John, *Ten Days That Shook the World* (New York: Vintage, 1960). Eyewitness account of the Revolution by the American journalist: part personal history, part myth making, it contains some beautifully written passages.

Serge, Victor, *Memoirs of a Revolutionary 1901–1941* (London: Oxford University Press, 1961). Extraordinary memoirs of a French revolutionary and novelist who joined the Bolshevik party and survived the Stalinist purges.

FICTION

Pasternak, Boris, *Dr. Zhivago* (New York: Knopf, 1991). Panoramic, if not melodramatic, description of Russia through revolution and civil war.

Serge, Victor, *Conquered City*. Richard Greeman, trans. (New York: Writers and Readers, 1978). Stirring novel of the Civil War that perfectly captures the tragedy of those events for the revolutionary dreams of 1917.

Solzhenitsyn, Alexander, *August 1914* (New York: Farrar, Straus & Giroux, 1972). Challenging novel about tsarist Russia's debacle in World War I. First volume of his *Red Wheel* epic.

FILMS ON VIDEO

Dr. Zhivago (1970)   Directed by David Lean and starring Julie Christie and Omar Sharif, a recreation of Boris Pasternak's famous novel.

October (1927)   Directed by the famous Russian filmmaker Sergei Eisenstein, a marvelous recounting of the Bolshevik's seizure of power in October, complete with the famous "storming" of the Winter Palace.

Reds (1980)   Directed by and starring Warren Beatty, a film biography of the American journalist and radical John Reed.

INDEX

Boldface numbers indicate major topics.
Italic numbers indicate illustrations.
Numbers followed by "m" indicate maps;
"c" indicates mention in the Chronology.

Brothers Karamazov, The (Fyodor Dostoevsky) 9
Bryant, Louise 107
Bulgaria 129
bureaucracy 4, 12
business elites (bourgeoisie) 10, 12–13,
  20

C

Cancer Ward (Alexander Solzhenitsyn)
  32
"carting out" 60
Catherine the Great (tsarina) 3
Chechen Republic 132–133
Cheka (Communist secret police) 117,
  118
Chekhov, Anton 8, 9–10
Chernenko, Constantin 129
Chernov, Viktor 21, 30, 69, 79
Cherry Orchard, The (Anton Chekhov)
  9–10
Chile 124
Cirque Moderne (Petrograd) 44m
Civil War (1918–20) 85, 115–121, 120m,
  137c
coalition government 55–67, 75
collectivization 128
Commonwealth of Independent States
  131
Comrade (ship) 72
Congress of Soviets 102, 104–105, 137c
Constantinople, Turkey 29
Constituent Assembly 23, 59, 112
Constitutional Democrats (Kadets) see
  also Miliukov, Paul
    founding of 13
    Kornilov Coup as discredit to 92
    Soviet opposed by 87
Cossacks 43, 45, 46
Council of Peoples Commissars 105, 137c
counterrevolutionaries (Whites) 111,
  115, 119, 121
Crime and Punishment (Fyodor Dosto-
  evsky) 9
Crimean War (1854–55) 6
czarist system see tsarist system
Czechoslovakia 129

D

Dardanelles 29
Dawn of Liberty (ship) 72
defense production 114
"defensist" factions (socialists) 30
demobilization 114

democracy 125
Development of Capitalism in Russia, The
  (Vladimir Lenin) 18
Devils, The (Fyodor Dostoevsky) 9
Dominican Republic 124
Dostoevsky, Fyodor 8–9
"dual power" 55–67
Duma (legislature)
  February Revolution dissolution of 47,
    49
  indictment of tsarism in 37
  weakness under tsar 24, 25
Duncan, Isadora 106
Durnovo, Peter 29

E

Eastern Europe 129, 130–131
East Germany 129
East Prussia 31
economic crisis
  after Revolution 113, 114, 119
  during Revolution 64, 75
  under tsarism 36
Ekaterinburg 120m
Emancipation Acts (1860) 7

F

factory committees 60, 114, 124, 125
famines 119, 128
farming see agriculture and farming
Fathers and Sons (Ivan Turgenev) 8
February Revolution (1917) 41–53, 44m,
  49, 135c
Field of Mars (Petrograd) 51
First Circle, The (Alexander Solzhenit-
  syn) 32
First Machine Gun Regiment 44m, 78
Five Year Plan 128
food shortages 64
Fortress of Peter and Paul (St. Peters-
  burg)
  February Revolution 48, 51, 52
  October Revolution 101, 104
France
  Russian Civil War intervention by 115
  in World War I 28, 30
Francis Ferdinand (archduke of Austria-
  Hungary) 27
Freud, Sigmund 106

G

Galicia 31
Gapon, Father 22

George, Lloyd 116
Germany
Brest Litovsk treaty 137c
reunification after Cold War 131
Russian Civil War intervention by 115
Russian revolutionaries funded by 84
Spartacist uprising 122
in World War I 28, 30, 31, 74, 98, 137c
glasnost (political openness) 130
Goldman, Emma 106
Golitsyn, Prince 47
Gorbachev, Mikhail 130, 131
Gorbachev, Raisa 130
Gorky, Maxim 50
Great Britain
Russian Civil War intervention by 115
in World War I 28, 30
Guatemala 124
Guchov, Alexander 58
Gulag Archipelago, The (Alexander
Solzhenitsyn) 32

H
hemophilia 35
Hungary 123, 129

I
Imperial Theater 1
industrialization *see* modernization
inflation 36, 76
intelligentsia 13, 24
International, Second 30
"internationalist" factions (socialists) 30
international revolution **122–124**
Italy 122

J
Japan 115 *see also* Russo-Japanese War
(1904–5)
Jews 117
judiciary 12
July Days (1917) 78–80, 79, 136c

K
Kadets *see* Constitutional Democrats
Kamenev, Lev 86, 97–99
Kazan Cathedral (St. Petersburg) 44m,
48
Kazan Square (St. Petersburg) 43
Kerensky, Alexander 57, **70**
June offensive ordered by 136c
Kornilov rivalry and coup 90–92

as minister of justice in Provisional Government 56
as minister of war in Provisional Government 69
October Revolution 103, 104, 136c
opposition to Petrograd Soviet 87
peasantry disillusioned with 88
plan to transfer Petrograd garrison 98,
99
second coalition government headed
by 86
Socialist Revolutionaries' support of terrorism 21
third coalition government headed by
93
unpreparedness for October Revolution 100–102
KGB (secret police) 131
Khabalov, General 46, 48
Khodynka Field Stampede (Moscow,
1894) 2–3
Khrushchev, Nikita 129
Kornilov, General Lavr 90–92, 136c
Kornilov Coup (August, 1917) 91–92,
136c
Kronstadt Revolt (1921) 126, 137c
Krupskaya, Nadezhda 18

L
land reform 88, 108, 114
Lenin (Vladimir Ulyanov) **18–19,** 62
call for insurrection by (September
1917) 96–98
Civil War 119
death and burial 127, 128
execution of brother by tsarist regime
17
in Finland 136c
march in honor of 127
membership in Russian Social Democratic Labor Party (RSDLP) 21
October Revolution 102, 103, 105, 108
pessimism while in exile 39
postrevolutionary government 112
Provisional Government charges
against 80, 83, 85, 86
return to Russia during February Revolution 61–64, 136c
rivalry with Trotsky 84
Leningrad *see* St. Petersburg
liberal democracy 12–13
liberals *see* Constitutional Democrats
Liebknecht, Karl 122
Liebman, Marcel 30, 85